The Atlantic City Gamble

A Twentieth Century Fund Report

The Twentieth Century Fund is an independent research foundation that undertakes policy studies of economic, political, and social institutions and issues. The Fund was founded in 1919 and endowed by Edward A. Filene.

A Twentieth Century Fund Report

THE
ATLANTIC CITY
GAMBLE

George
Sternlieb

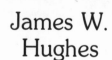

James W.
Hughes

Harvard University Press
Cambridge, Massachusetts, and London, England   1983

Library of Congress Cataloging in Publication Data

Sternlieb, George.
The Atlantic City gamble.

"A Twentieth Century Fund report."
Includes bibliographical references and index.
1. Gambling—New Jersey—Atlantic City. 2. Gambling—
Economic aspects—New Jersey—Atlantic City. 3. Atlantic
City (N.J.)—Social conditions. I. Hughes, James W.
II. Title.
HV6721.A8S73   1983   338.4'7795'0974985   83-8375
ISBN 0-674-05125-4

ACKNOWLEDGMENTS

The saga of Atlantic City's involvement with casinos sprawls through time and indeed, particularly when one is looking for sources, through space. Assembling it would have been impossible without the help of a most talented group of research associates. Clifford B. Meier provided insights into the history of the city, its politics, and its people in a fashion that confirms our impression of him as a most talented young historian. Robert Rutter was responsible for the general history of gambling and the preliminary rites of passage of the casino legislation. Richard Lehne's unique competence in appraising both the immediacies of the 1976 legislation—and the ensuing confusion that took place in terms of administrative mechanisms—was most valuable and is reflected in Chapter 4; the full-scale monograph that he has in preparation will be a major contribution to the field. Michael Hawkins selflessly shared with us his ongoing research in terms of the housing picture. In addition, Charles Tantillo of Stockton State College provided insights into the immediacies of the environment and the impact that the casinos have had on the city's population.

They were joined in these endeavors by the superbly talented librarian at the Rutgers University Center for Urban Policy Research, Edward Duensing, whose broad bibliographic insights into the range of materials, both in the gaming press as well as in more learned areas, are only partly reflected in the book. He tirelessly ensured consistency and an orderly flow of information.

Our editors, Chris Farrell and Beverly Goldberg of the Twentieth Century Fund, were both merciless critics—and splendidly helpful friends. Mary Picarella, publications director of the Center for Urban Policy Research, maintained structure over a drowning pool of data and supervised the creative typing and in-house editing of our staff people, Lydia Lombardi and Joan Frantz.

We were beneficiaries of the enthusiastic cooperation of many experts in the field. We would like to single out particularly the gambler's paladin, Walter Tyminski, editor of *Rouge et Noir*. The editors of *Gambling Business Magazine* and the casino experts of the accounting firm of Laventhol and Horwath were most generous. Our thanks also go to the several stock market advisory services that shared information with us.

We are grateful to the many individuals who were interviewed in the course of the study, some anonymously, others noted in the text, without whose help the work would have been far less complete. Last but far from least, we would like to acknowledge the support of the Twentieth Century Fund and the guidance provided by Murray J. Rossant and Gary Nickerson, whose insights and patient prodding were most useful.

The book is dedicated to the use of the bewildered promoter, voter, and official who contemplate "going Atlantic City."

CONTENTS

FOREWORD

The quest for a quick and painless, that is, politically popular, means of raising funds and stimulating economic development never ends. In the last decade, politicians seized on a number of seemingly ingenious devices, from lotteries to off-track betting, that promised benefits such as big increases in revenues and decreases in the role of so-called organized crime. The results have rarely measured up to the expectations—the only thing painless about lotteries and betting shops is the way in which they have parted their clients from their money, and the only real benefits have been to the relatively few individuals who have hit large jackpots and the politicians who have found a new and rich source of patronage.

Legalized casino gambling is the latest of the solutions to beguile politicians. For many years, Nevada was the only state with legalized gaming, and because of its relatively small population and its distance from major urban centers, it was not really seen as a model worth emulating. But when the campaign to legalize gambling in the fading seaside resort of Atlantic City, New Jersey, got under way, gambling was billed as a sort of magic bullet that would spur growth and lower unemployment, transforming a blighted city in the process.

The Twentieth Century Fund, which has a continuing program of support for studies of urban problems, particularly examinations of the fiscal problems facing America's older urban areas, was very interested in these developments in Atlantic City. It seemed likely that, if the legalization referendum passed, other cities would be tempted to follow the same path. Therefore, during the campaign for legalization in the early 1970s, the Fund, along with the Fund for the City of New York, set up an independent Task Force to examine the issue. The referendum was defeated, but the supporters of the idea did not give up.

Later, after a second referendum passed, Atlantic City became a laboratory case of what gaming could mean for economic growth. A few years later, George Sternlieb, head of the Center for Urban Policy Research of Rutgers University, approached the Fund with a proposal on Atlantic City and its experience with legalized gambling. He had access to a considerable body of data on Atlantic City that had been gathered by the Center, and the assistance of James W. Hughes, who had closely followed developments there. An attractive proposal for the Fund, it was presented to the Trustees, who gave their approval.

Sternlieb and Hughes have provided a detailed balance sheet on the experiment in Atlantic City. They raise serious questions that go beyond economic issues and show the political and social costs that accompany the establishment of casino gambling. This study should give other states and cities, especially in decaying resort areas, looking to legalized gambling as a possible answer to their problems, pause for thought. What they have done is make it absolutely clear that the effects of gambling as a state-sanctioned activity ought to be subject to public debate.

George Sternlieb and James W. Hughes have provided an analytical framework that allows us to assess the role of legalized gambling as a means of economic revitalization, and they have also explored those social issues raised by legalization that must be considered by policymakers and the public. The Fund is grateful to them for their efforts.

M. J. Rossant, Director
The Twentieth Century Fund
April 1983

The Atlantic City Gamble

THE SEMIMAGIC BULLET

1

Gambling, Atlantic City style: The bus burrows through the Pinelands that surround what used to be one of America's grandest seashore resorts, speeds past the bleak reality of present-day Atlantic City, of vacant stores and empty lots, and pulls up at the loading dock of the casino. The people come out of the bus carefully holding the grab bars, dismounting stiffly. In part their timidity reflects this new experience – riding the gaming bus two hours from Newark to Atlantic City and suddenly being faced with a glittering casino; in part it reflects concern for elderly bodies, for indeed they are elderly. This particular busload represents the membership of a church-organized Golden Age club. About two-thirds are women, noticeably more vigorous than the men aboard the bus, but the men seem filled with instant machismo and grim-faced determination to return with, if not big winnings, then tales of how close they came.

They have paid $14 for the bus trip but receive $5 for lunch and $10 in change for the slots. Once inside, in the perpetual twi-

light of the casinos, the bus travelers look vaguely ethereal, all of them clutching white paper cups filled with coins for the machines that take up nearly half the casino floor. There is no place to sit down, a major problem for the elderly. Rumor has it that the lack of seats is part of an industry ploy to get Keno into the casinos; then the elderly can sit and play at the same time.

A few of the people empty their cups of change and move outside to sit on the boardwalk, reminisce about the good old days, and watch the ocean. But the average bus visitor will lose $20 out of pocket, at a marginal cost to the casinos of about $6 to $8. The charter buses account for nearly half of the total visitors to the casinos, and about 30 percent of them – in a good month, more than 250,000 – are the elderly. They have a good time and come back for more. There is an animal vitality to the casinos, and maybe it doesn't matter that it's a losing game.

The state of New Jersey officially embarked upon a "great experiment" in November 1976, when the electorate approved a referendum amending the state's constitution to authorize gambling in Atlantic City. The casino gaming industry was expected to transform a dying city core into an exciting resort and convention center. Employment in Atlantic City would swell. The city's tax base would broaden. Tourism would spread throughout the state. Welfare rolls would diminish. The cruel spectacle of a poverty-stricken community attempting to support its poor with inadequate local resources would be eliminated. Moreover, state taxes on casino gambling revenues were earmarked to provide a new source of needed money for state-sponsored programs to help the elderly.

Whether or not these expectations were too great, the huge volume of business at Atlantic City's casinos has stimulated interest in legalized gambling in other states that are short of revenues and have depressed resort areas in need of the economic benefits that casinos seem to bestow. Even before the full magnitude of the revenue Atlantic City could generate was apparent, at least eight other states in the Northeast and smokestack areas of the Midwest were seriously considering legalizing casino gaming.[1] These states, particularly New York,

Connecticut, Pennsylvania, and Massachusetts, are now review-
ing all the supposed benefits of legalized gambling. In recent
years, these and most other states in the Northeast have regarded
legalized lotteries and, in some cases, off-track betting as a good
source of government funds. Casinos seem to offer even richer
rewards.

Climate of Acceptance

A few years ago, the idea that an American electorate would accept legalization of casino gaming on a broad scale would have
been judged highly unlikely at best. The factors that led to the
shift are varied, but principal among them are a desperate need to
stimulate economic growth, especially in urban settings and ob-
solete resort areas; the fiscal squeeze that is strangling governmental bodies at all levels; the growing belief that gambling cannot be controlled by outlawing it; and a significant change in
public attitudes toward gaming.

In the United States the drive for economic growth and/or
revitalization has become a primary concern of governments and
their electorates. The sense of economic insecurity arises out of
competition from Japan as well as from some of the European
nations. In the slow-growth regions of the country, particularly
the Northeast and Midwest, the fact that the South and the West
are securing an increasing flow of population, jobs, and with them
tax capacity adds to the anxiety. The older areas are being left
behind. Frequently they find themselves faced with the need to
provide greater and greater levels of social benefits in their core
areas from a steadily decreasing tax base.

The fight for the creation of new jobs is a bitter and costly one.
It is estimated that the state of Pennsylvania took on obligations of
a quarter of a billion dollars to secure a Volkswagen assembly
plant within its boundaries. Similarly, Nissan, the manufacturer of
Datsun automobiles and trucks, in return for locating its assembly
facilities in Tennessee, secured a $15 million site improvement, a
substantial tax exemption, the rezoning of 2,200 peripheral acres
for heavy industry, and a development whose plant was aided by

a $450 million bond issue. As a final touch, the state subsidized a trip to Japan by 800 supervisory employees for training prior to the opening of the facility – and all this for perhaps 6,000 jobs.[2] Compare Atlantic City's 29,000 new jobs in four years (with little start-up cost to the state), and the allure of casinos is obvious.

In many cases, fiscal desperation on the part of public bodies makes for an easy acceptance of gaming. Income-tax increases are unpopular; sales-tax increments are difficult to secure and may shift retail sales to areas with lower sales taxes or none at all. The seeming ease of sharing in the largess generated by gaming in all of its forms is politically appealing. In New Jersey, the path to casino gaming was smoothed by an increasing acceptance of state government reliance on gambling as a significant source of funds. By 1979, net state revenues from lotteries in the United States had risen to almost a billion dollars, and pari-mutuel taxes amounted to over three-quarters of a billion.[3]

Certainly, when politicians looked at the example of Nevada, the potential of securing some share of casino revenues was hard to resist. More than one out of every three dollars spent by that state come from taxes on gaming. And the basic vigor of the source seemed inexorable. In the decade of the 1970s, the annual growth rate in the gaming win of Las Vegas was 16.9 percent, and this growth rate was achieved in a period in which many of America's basic industries showed little or no growth.[4]

Illegal gambling generates corruption, particularly in large city police forces. The final report of the federal Commission on the Review of the National Policy Toward Gambling (CRNPTG) states that a survey of 298 large city police departments showed that, within the five years from 1972 to 1976, 17 percent had investigated officers for legal misconduct in connection with gambling enforcement,[5] and in a majority of the investigations the defendants were found guilty.

Experts have frequently pointed out that police involvement in gambling payoffs, often referred to by officers as "clean graft," can lead to involvement in other forms of corruption. Once the police accept money for the protection of gambling operations, it is more difficult to refuse it for narcotics dealing and other crimes.

The conclusion of the CRNPTG final report is simple: "effective gambling law enforcement is impossible . . . How can any law which prohibits what 80 percent of the people approve of be enforced?" The answer proposed by the commission and an increasing proportion of national officialdom is to legalize, to regulate, and to tax gambling. The commission report is worth citing:

> Current gambling policy on the state level accurately reflects the ambivalence and contradiction that has traditionally characterized this nation's approach to gamblers over the years. Strong conflicting sentiments surface: gambling is a morally and socially destructive activity that must be suppressed, and that the enormous popularity of gambling makes it a suitable activity for governments to channel – through licensing and taxation. In the current year of economic distress combined with increased toleration of once proscribed activities, the lure of illegal gambling revenues prompted a number of states to reexamine state gambling policies with a view toward legalization.[6]

In other words, if you can't lick 'em, join 'em!

Tolerance is replacing hostility toward state involvement in gaming. This conversion, national in scope, is puzzling in a period that is also characterized by a swing toward religious fundamentalism. It appears that the mission of wealthy elites to act as moral adjudicators of the behavior of the poor, which marked the reform waves of earlier eras, is much more selectively applied today. The antigaming forces of the period between the two world wars were dominated by a coalition of church groups and the social and economic elite. Although this alliance is far from dead, it is much less vigorous than it once was.

The tide of Puritan morality, a belief not merely in following the path of virtue oneself but in showing one's neighbor the way, which results in the broad external imposition of moral values, seems to have receded – at least in regard to gambling. Surveys conducted in the early 1970s indicated that Protestants as a group, particularly those affiliated with churches, held negative attitudes toward gaming, while the attitudes of Jews and Catholics were much more positive.[7] In 1978, a Gallup poll concluded that actual exposure to and participation in casino gaming by Protestants and Catholics were nearly equal.[8] Differences in the results of the two surveys must be viewed in light of the fact that one stressed attitudes and the other stressed behavior. Even so, it is safe to infer an increased level of tolerance toward gambling among Protestants.

Whatever the reasons behind the decline of late nineteenth-century and early twentieth-century reform movements, the result is a greater acceptance of gaming activity. In a "play" society dedicated to leisure-time pursuits, or at least to the publicizing of them, gaming is merely seen as one more form of entertainment to be purchased with discretionary income. Gamblers Anonymous may rail about the dangers this outlet holds for the compulsive, but few people automatically view the occasional bettor as a bad credit risk.

Within the past decade, the major hotel chains have moved into the gaming industry. Today, gaming participation by hotel chains has become a large positive factor in corporate market evaluations. For example, Dean Witter Reynolds' *Lodging Industry Periodical*, a highly respected stock-market report, highlights the relative attractiveness of the Hilton Hotels and Holiday Inns as gaming companies.[9] It is particularly noteworthy that Holiday is commended for having finally committed itself (at the cost of losing some of its more moralistic managers) to casino gambling with its purchase of Harrah's. This is in contrast to the example of the Marriott Corporation, which the report cites as "one of the class operators in the lodging industry. However, the firm has repeatedly stated that it 'wants no part of the gaming industry.'" In Dean Witter's market analysis, such a decision is viewed in a negative light.[10]

The growing acceptability of casino gaming (as well as its less positive history) is illustrated by the statement of James E. Ritchie, formerly the director of the United States Gambling Commission, at a conference sponsored by the leading hotel and restaurant accounting firm of Laventhol and Horwath in 1979: "Remember just 20 years ago a meeting to discuss casino gambling might well have been held in a back room in Appalachia, not at the Waldorf Astoria in the public eye."[11]

Nevada as Prototype

The Nevada experience has dominated discussion of the form and organization of proposed casino development in all other states. It has also been used to define problems of governance. The sheer profitability and scale of the casinos in Nevada has obscured other possible approaches, including state operation. For casinos on the Las Vegas strip, for example, average return on equity capital was 26.3 percent from 1967 to 1975; this figure was substantially lower than the equivalent for the lower-class casinos in downtown Las Vegas, where annual rates of return were in excess of 40 percent of equity. In other words, the payback period on investments in downtown casinos was two and a half years. The Lake Tahoe casinos and those in Reno averaged approximately a three-year payback period.[12]

An estimated quarter of all jobs in the state of Nevada comes directly from gaming industries and the related tourist industries. Furthermore, Governor Robert List of Nevada estimated that an additional quarter of all business employment in the state is directly dependent upon the gaming industry. Governor List could point out that in 1980, with gaming as a principal contributor to the state's tax base, Nevada had no corporate income tax, inheritance tax, or personal income tax, and had no general tax increase since 1969.[13] Given the tax pressures that are building throughout the country, this is no small benefit. The vigor of the casinos in Nevada is indicated by the awesome fact that the state's take of $193 million in 1981 represented barely one-thirteenth of the industry's more than $2.5 billion in gross win.

Nevada has set the pattern for current approaches to casino gambling within the United States. In the words of a former commissioner of the New Jersey Control Commission, "It is Nevada that provided the matrix of credit in the casinos, of heavy entertainment to attract clientele, and of the overall creation of an ambiance that has to be seen to be believed, of a casino hooded from the rest of the world – a world unto itself."[14] Nevada's gaming is a success because of the massive pulling power of its critical assemblage of gaming facilities and their widespread publicity.

The Nevada casinos have perfected several techniques for attracting clients. These include packaging trips for potential gamers, subsidizing transportation costs on bus lines and charter flights, working with travel agencies that bring tour groups into the state, and selling the state as an ideal convention site. These techniques serve as a guide to other locations.

The characteristics of Nevada gaming patrons give some insight into the reality. Gambling is far and away the most important reason for visiting Las Vegas, with a typical stay on the order of slightly less than four days. Data collected in 1976, the year New Jersey was moving toward a positive decision on legalized casino gambling, show that nearly one out of seven visitors had an income of less than $10,000. An additional one out of five had an income from $10,000 to $15,000. Roughly one-third of the visitors had a total family income of less than $15,000.[15]

It is conventions that bring in the higher-income groups. Thirty percent of the convention visitors in 1976 had incomes of over $40,000. Their average expenditures while in Las Vegas that year were $86 per day exclusive of gaming. This figure is fully a third higher than that for expenditures of all visitors.

Despite its reputation as a national and international playground, more than half of the visitors to Las Vegas in 1976 came from the West, an additional 19 percent from the Midwest, and only about 11 to 12 percent from the East and South. Even in its isolated location, which makes it unlikely that people casually stop in, propinquity played a major role in decisions to go there.

In addition, Nevadans themselves gamble more than most Americans. In 1974, 78 percent of Nevada residents placed some sort of bet as compared with 61 percent across the nation. Those between the ages of twenty-five and sixty-four were the most frequent gamblers at casinos, with more men than women and more blacks than whites, on a proportional basis, among the bettors. Above the age of sixty-four, the percentage of casino bettors drops sharply. In a study conducted by the National Gambling Commission, only 3.6 percent of people who had bet in casinos were over the age of sixty-four. The commission also found that gambling in Nevada was regressive, meaning that lower-income groups spent a higher proportion of their incomes on gambling.[16]

A number of commentators think that the isolation of Las Vegas has been critical to the success of gaming. A local scholar, William R. Eadington, has raised the question of why other states do not legalize gambling, since from an economic standpoint the Nevada experiment is an overwhelming success. His conclusion is that "for casino gambling to be economically successful, it needs to draw tourists as its main customers [otherwise it merely consumes locally derived incomes]. It is unlikely that this objective can be fulfilled unless the casinos are spatially separated from the major markets. To locate the casinos in urban areas will probably lead to exclusively lower-income casinos which are undesirable because of the lack of revenues they are capable of generating as well as the high social cost they might create."[17] But this is a warning that was not heeded by New Jersey; nor has it been completely explored by some of the other heavily urbanized states that are considering gaming.

The Atlantic City Reality

The decisions made in regard to legalization of casino gambling must be based on a set of facts as comprehensive and accurate as possible. Far too often, as was the case in New Jersey, public policy decisions have been generated on the basis of exaggerated claims, inadequate analyses, and wishful thinking. But there can now be a sound basis for policymaking: the Atlantic City experiment can be carefully studied and a rational framework constructed. Such an analysis will help other states to decide whether they should legalize gambling and, if so, under what conditions.

Atlantic City is not the Poconos of Pennsylvania, the burnt-out urban core of New York City's Far Rockaway, or any of the other half hundred dying resort locations that have been suggested as potential sites for casinos. It is, however, practically a prototype of the decayed resort area with aging infrastructure, diminished job base, and poor capacity to raise taxes in the face of overwhelming need. Understanding the effect of legalized casino gambling on Atlantic City provides a very useful starting point for other jurisdictions contemplating similar steps.

The scorecard of winners and losers since Resorts International, the first of Atlantic City's legal gambling palaces, opened its doors in 1978 can be stated very simply: the booming casino business in New Jersey is evident, but legalization of gambling has had negative results as well, among them increased activity by organized crime and a toll in human and economic displacement.

Obscured by enormous construction cost overruns, bad management, and cries of woe calculated to lift some of the restrictions initially placed on them, investment in the casinos has proven to be highly remunerative. From the outset, the volume of revenues and profits in Atlantic City's casinos exceeded even the most optimistic expectations, which had been based in large part on the Nevada experience. But Atlantic City had the advantage of being the only legal gambling market in a densely populated region. There were 50 million people who could leave their homes in the morning, spend the day at the casinos, and return home the same night.

Between May 26, 1978, and the end of 1981, nine casinos began operating, representing an investment of well over $1 billion. By the end of 1982, the city's casinos had approached the $3.7 billion mark in cumulative gross revenue from gambling since its inception.[18] The average monthly take per casino in the summer of 1982 approached the $15 million level, and Resorts International alone passed the $1 billion mark in February 1983.

Even the bleak month of February 1981, when a downturn in casino business was stirring fear and confusion in New Jersey, Caesars Boardwalk Regency and the Golden Nugget generated average daily wins in excess of $10 per square foot of casino space. It would take a productive shopping center about three months to generate an equivalent gross margin. Atlantic City's casinos, therefore, are roughly one hundred times more profitable per square foot than a shopping center. (A 40,000-square-foot casino has a gross margin production equivalent to four major regional shopping centers of a million square feet each.)

The casinos have generated a substantial growth in new jobs. Currently, nine casinos directly employ nearly 30,000 workers. There has been, however, amazingly little spillover growth into noncasino employment within Atlantic City. The absolute number of unemployed in the city has not changed appreciably. There is some indication of a decline in Atlantic City's heavy welfare rolls. But still in September 1981, more than one in eleven of the total county population were receiving support from the Aid to Families with Dependent Children program.

The new jobs that the casinos created have been more fruitful for suburban residents outside the city than for those within it. The absolute number of employed in the region as a whole has clearly grown. Yet the absolute number of unemployed especially in Atlantic City, but also within Atlantic County, has remained remarkably constant. The employment situation for the citizens of Atlantic City is far from the millennium that had been pledged, despite the casinos' practical monopoly in a region of 50 million people.

Since legalization, housing values have soared, which may be splendid for owners but a disaster for the underhoused population. Atlantic City's total assessed land values are now higher than Newark's, a city with eight times as many residents.[19] But the visitor to the city who passes beyond the thin layer of tinsel trappings along the boardwalk enters a wasteland with perhaps less economic activity than there was before the casinos. There can be no question that the city's stock of affordable and adequate housing declined after the casinos came.

Nothing of consequence has been done to improve the poor housing conditions that predate legalization. Moreover, the casinos themselves and the land speculation fever that followed them have caused large-scale displacement, and nothing has been done to relieve the hardships that displacement causes. Atlantic City may not have been the best of all refuges for the elderly before legalization, but now even the dismal comforts that it afforded are being swept away. The situation for minority groups is even worse. While some have benefited from casino employment, all too many have seen their homes fall into uninhabitable disrepair or burned down by landlords hoping to profit from rampant land speculation. Arson is not unique to Atlantic City, but the extent of the profit to property owners through its use may well be.

The state secured more than $117 million in taxes in 1982 from the casinos, but the projected bonanza to Atlantic City, based on local property taxes, has been largely offset by the stresses on the municipal treasury that the casinos have brought in their wake. In other words, a large percentage of the taxes paid by the casinos to the city is absorbed by the municipal services they require, particularly public safety. There is evidence that the city will have to make major investments in the development and improvement of its infrastructure in order to create the amenities needed to compete with other resort areas. A vast convention hall must be financed; municipal services are clearly inadequate and must be upgraded and expanded; and housing conditions must be improved. The nominal revenue increases that appear on the Atlantic City balance sheet from casino taxation may be substantially overstated in light of the city's growing fiscal expenditures.

Part of the rationale for legalized gambling is that it provides competition for illegal gaming. There is significant evidence that this is not the case. Gambling of any kind encourages more gambling. Far from feeling the sting of competition, illegal operations find more clients. But it is crime and corruption, not increased illegal gambling, which now worries the residents of Atlantic City and the state of New Jersey. In Atlantic City, street crime has run rampant, and prostitution has become so widespread that the city's chief of police, in despair of curbing it, recommended that it be legalized.

Perhaps most detrimental is the vast potential for corruption nourished by the very presence of the casinos. The web of licensing requirements and the catastrophic costs of losing a license create a need for casino operators to cultivate powerful friends in government. The nature of casino gambling makes it particularly susceptible to skimming, or the removal of a portion of the earnings before reporting them to the regulatory authorities. Therefore, gaming interests are potentially able to create massive secret funds to buy political influence and patronage.

Organized crime may or may not be behind current management and ownership of the casinos. There can be no question, however, of its significant infiltration into the service industries and labor unions in the city. If licensing requirements are stringent enough to prevent organized crime from using the front door, then it will come in through the back door.

Lost in the debate over the casinos' relative virtues (or lack of them) is a clear view of who ultimately pays the tab for their facilities, some of which cost more than $300 million to build and have among the highest-paid executives in American industry. The state's over $100 million a year take is not without cost – and much of this cost is paid by those least able to bear the burden.

Atlantic City as a family resort, projected as one of the goals of legalization, has never materialized. Unless conditions change radically, it probably never will. The daytripper rather than the overnight visitor dominates the scene, distinguishing Atlantic City from relatively isolated Nevada. By a very rough estimate, charter-bus patrons account for nearly half of the total visitors to the casinos. In a good month, more than 20,000 buses will bring passengers to the casinos from adjoining areas in a three-hundred-mile radius. Approximately 30 percent of the total occupants of these buses (more than 250,000 people) are the elderly.[20]

Competing casinos use relatively standard methods to attract bus patrons. Casinos lease buses to transport patrons. Transportation from New York, for example, costs the casino $5 to $6 per passenger. Each passenger is charged $15. The bulk of the fare is reimbursed by the casino, and in some cases a low-cost or free lunch is provided as well. Many anecdotes are told about canny old people who use the excursions as a no-cost outing, "brown-bagging it" on the boardwalk and avoiding the casinos' lures. In fact, the average bus patron loses $20 at the casino, netting the casino from $12 to $14 after out-of-pocket expenses.

Casino gambling in Atlantic City is far from an export industry. For every dollar secured by the state through the gaming tax, based on an 8 percent tax on a casino's gross win, patrons, 40 percent of whom are New Jersey residents, must lose $12.50. Assuming that New Jersey residents bet as heavily as out-of-state visitors suggests a $5 loss by residents of the state for *every total* gaming tax dollar that goes to the state treasury (40 percent of $12.50).

A Better Way?

Why has the New Jersey experiment had such checkered results? Are the problems merely those of faulty organization and administration, or are they an organic part of casino gaming itself? Certainly the forms of governance have been far from perfect. The state endorsed visions of glorious rebirth, but it failed to provide a governing mechanism that could produce the promised results. There has been a constant tug-of-war between the state's desire to maximize its share of the take, which was to be used for the public good, and the casinos' protestations that taxes must be maintained at a moderate level and governance standards relaxed if the industry is to grow.

The immediate success of the casinos created expectations for future growth that completely undermined realistic efforts to achieve the goals that had been articulated before legalization. Instant success brought the casinos political clout, and any major reshaping of the casinos' contribution was foreclosed.

While New Jersey's state government alternates between glee at over $100 million a year in relatively painless (at least from a politician's point of view) tax revenue and regret that it did not demand an even larger share of the take, there is barely a ripple on the local level to reflect any positive result. The unemployed remain substantially unemployed; the tourists stay within the encapsulated world of the casinos; the older retailing and service sectors of the community continue to degenerate.

The time when municipalities could survive by seeking aid from federal and state governments is coming to an end, a victim of the taxpayers' revolt. Local bootstrapping is the order of the day in an atmosphere of increasing fiscal and economic fear. So localities will increasingly reexamine gaming as a potential source of economic and fiscal well-being. The Atlantic City experience will be mined for information on what to do and what not to do.

THE STATE AND GAMBLING

Americans have always gambled for recreation, and governments have alternately legalized gambling to raise tax revenues and prohibited it when crime and corruption stirred public outrage. Even during the colonial era, moral and legal debates over gambling were commonplace. The Puritans were strongly opposed to gambling on religious and moral grounds and, within a decade of the Mayflower landing, strict antigambling legislation was enacted. Massachusetts and Connecticut banned lotteries, dice, and cards in the 1670s. But gambling was acceptable in the southern colonies. Horse racing was particularly popular in Virginia. The few gambling laws passed in the southern colonies were limited in impact. The contrast between Virginia and Massachusetts colonies mirrors the pro- and antigambling tensions of present-day America and the different viewpoints on the role of government in gambling.

For state government officials, the allure of legalized gambling has always been raising painless tax revenue, especially when a neighboring state is the source of much of the gaming money. A classic element in selling legalized gaming is to link its tax receipts to some highly popular good cause. Moral qualms against gaming, therefore, can be shrewdly twisted into arguments against the sick or the old or education. In most instances, however, expected tax revenues have rarely come close to the figures suggested during legalization efforts. If the state's share was less than expected, so was the portion assigned to special needs.

Moreover, throughout the long history of gambling in America, state governments have hoped that legalization will preempt illegal activity. Although this has been shown to be an illusion, the argument is continually resurrected. It is the age-old linkage of crime and criminals to gambling that leads to repeated reform efforts to curb or suppress legalized gaming. So New Jersey's legalization of casino gambling is only the most recent event in this history of weighing the benefits and costs to the state of sanctioned gaming.

Lotteries

In colonial America, many states regarded lotteries as a legitimate method of fundraising for charitable organizations, schools, and businesses. Although such lotteries were extremely popular, they did not always achieve their goal of acquiring adequate funds for the sponsoring organization. Institutions that used lotteries in an attempt to meet their budgets, notably early American universities such as Princeton and Rutgers, often had to resort to fundraising expeditions to England and Holland.[1]

During the first part of the nineteenth century, government did little to suppress gambling and, in some cases, became involved in it as a means of raising revenue. In 1831, for example, eight East Coast states collected over $53 million through lotteries. In relation to state budgets, which were very small in this period, this sum was quite significant.[2]

Lotteries of the early nineteenth century were soon tainted by corruption. As successive scandals were publicized, antilottery groups called for investigations and suppression. Legislative measures aimed at reforming the lotteries failed to stop the irregularities, and antilottery laws were passed by many states in the late 1830s.[3]

A generation later, during the financial chaos in the American South that followed the Civil War, lotteries enjoyed a resurgence. Money was scarce; lending institutions were few; and state coffers were dry. Louisiana's new constitution allowed the state to license lotteries and gambling houses, and in August 1869 a private lottery company was established. The Louisiana Lottery Company was required to pay $40,000 a year to the state to finance the Charity Hospital in New Orleans. The use of profits from gambling for charitable causes is an established tactic to ensure its acceptance within the community.

The lottery proved popular beyond expectation. Dazzled by this success, the state began to license gambling houses. Casinos flourished and spread. Abuses by licensed gambling houses were rampant, and the number of illegal casinos continued to grow. The illegal casino operators, under the guise of reform, were instrumental in finally generating enough pressure on local politicians in New Orleans to force repeal of the licensing law, thereby reducing the competition. This action did not lead to the demise of gambling; instead, a system of police bribes and back-alley deals seemed to control gambling better than legalization.[4]

In contrast to the failure of licensed gambling houses, the lottery company succeeded magnificently. After raising funds on the New Orleans stock exchange, the company expanded rapidly. Soon every state in the Union was flooded with its tickets. Daily, monthly, and semiannual drawings, along with clever promotion, aroused national interest. It became increasingly clear that the company was in violation of numerous state and federal statutes; but, through the liberal use of bribes, the New Orleans lottery flourished. Its moment, however, was passing; opposition by a growing number of concerned citizens throughout the country, lawsuits, and new federal legislation began to strangle the enterprise. But even with these regulatory efforts, the lottery expired only when its twenty-five-year charter ended.[5]

The experience with the Louisiana Lottery Company resulted in a firm national resolve among reformers and some politicians to prohibit gambling. The federal government enacted legislation designed to cut off the lifeblood of state lotteries. Effective laws, however, evolved slowly. Dozens of acts regulating the use of the mails for lottery material were passed between 1864 and 1890, but such legislation had loopholes that defeated their purpose until 1890, when a stronger bill was passed. Lottery tickets could no longer be sent through the mails, but they could still be carried across state lines. Interstate transportation of lottery material was finally made illegal in 1895. The combined effect of these federal statutes was to eliminate state lotteries for the next seventy years.[6]

By the early 1960s, the possibility of securing revenues from gaming once more appealed to states faced with expanding budgets and limited resources. New Hampshire was the first state to resurrect the lottery as a means of public finance. The state had endured an ongoing fiscal crisis because its politicians refused to impose a sales tax or an income tax. In desperation, the legislature turned to a lottery to provide economic salvation for New Hampshire schools.[7] Proponents excitedly projected a net of over $4 million annually, with each school in the state to receive a flat grant per student. New Hampshire implemented the lottery in 1964 with high expectations, but it took ten years to realize the original projections, and net receipts have, for the most part, stayed between $3 million and $4 million since that time.

The reasons for New Hampshire's limited success are varied, and enough of them have to do with how this particular lottery was run so that the reputation of the lottery as an alternative to other forms of taxation was not seriously damaged. New Hampshire charged a high $3 price per ticket and initially held only one drawing a year, although the state did move toward cheaper tickets and more frequent drawings. Perhaps the riskiest part of the whole lottery scheme in New Hampshire was its complete dependence on nonresident support. If every New Hampshire citizen had bought one ticket (and no tickets had been sold to outsiders), the gross take would not have equaled the prizes paid out.[8] Fortunately, a high percentage of the tickets, over 80 percent in 1964, were purchased by nonresidents, mostly from Massachusetts, New York, and Connecticut.

More tickets might have been sold to out-of-state buyers if they were not forced to travel to New Hampshire to obtain tickets; federal law still prohibited the use of the mail for lottery purposes. In addition, the Federal Communications Commission (FCC) was enforcing a federal statute forbidding television or radio advertising of lotteries. But this limitation was soon put to rest as the pressure for expanding gaming grew more intense.

Even though New Hampshire was only modestly successful in raising funds with a state lottery, New York quickly followed its example. The argument was that the New Hampshire lottery was siphoning New York money out of the state. Why not stop the flow and relieve some fiscal problems at the same time? The classic assertion that gambling taxes are painless made the lottery appear even more attractive. In state after state, the justifications for legalized gaming are always the same: It is a painless form of taxation; all the other states are doing it and are gaining earmarked funds for a good cause, whether it be education, the elderly, or hospitals. Why shouldn't we?

Like New Hampshire residents, New Yorkers were told that the receipts of the lottery would be used for a most worthy purpose: education. The shallowness of this commitment became apparent when, after the first year of operation, lottery receipts were diverted into the general fund because of a year-end budget squeeze. New Yorkers were informed that the lottery could yield $360 million in its first year. To achieve this figure every New York resident would have had to lose $20 on the lottery. The net yield never came close to these original estimates. The addition of new "games" brought the total revenue take as late as 1982 to only half of the original projection. And even this required scrapping of all the nominal safeguards of minimum bet and restriction of selling place. The belief in a passive legal substitute successfully competing with illegal gaming was quietly forgotten. New York was quick to blame the lottery's failure on the federal law banning mass media advertising and federal restrictions on the use of the mails. The growing evidence that lotteries were simply a limited fundraising method was ignored.[9]

While New York was experimenting with a lottery and off-track betting (OTB), New Jersey legislators, as the 1960s drew to a close, were facing fiscal problems of their own. The Assembly was trying to avoid instituting a state income tax, the revenue-producing method favored by Governor William Cahill. The legislature bemoaned the fact that New York and New Hampshire were cashing in on a lottery while New Jersey was not. Once again, the fear of losing funds to neighboring states that have legalized gambling was used in its support. This argument, of course, conveniently overlooked the fact that neither state lottery could be deemed a great success. Legislators simply saw what they believed to be millions of New Jersey dollars escaping the state to its northern neighbors.

New Jerseyans have a history of approving various legalized gambling proposals. Pari-mutuel horse betting was legalized in 1939. The most recent New Jersey constitution, adopted in 1947, included the pari-mutuel betting provision, as well as a clause specifying that voters had to pass judgment on any gambling measure through referendum. In 1953, New Jerseyans voted to allow bingo and raffles by nonprofit groups for charitable purposes. In 1959, voters passed a referendum ratifying the Amusement Games Licensing Law, which permitted amusement parks and resorts to operate games of chance. This act was extended in 1961 to cover agricultural fairs.[10] In all cases, the introduction of these games in a given municipality was contingent on approval in a local referendum.

In 1964 and again in 1966, attempts were made to establish OTB and a lottery in the state. Neither was approved by the legislature. But the passage of the New York and New Hampshire lotteries, combined with legislators' desire to avoid an income tax, spurred further attempts to institute a New Jersey lottery. Proponents argued that a lottery would net over $200 million. The profits of the lottery, later mandated at 40 percent of the gross take, were to support education throughout the state. The legislature finally approved a referendum for the ballot in 1970. The lottery was approved and established.[11]

Compared with New York and New Hampshire, the New Jersey lottery was enormously successful. (See Table 1 at the back of the book.) But this success was at the cost of many of the safeguards originally included in the New York and New Hampshire lotteries that aimed at limiting losses by the poor.

New Hampshire tickets went for $3 for a semiannual drawing and a prize of $50,000. New York charged $1 per ticket for both a monthly and a triannual drawing with top prizes of $100,000 and $250,000, respectively. New Jersey started with a $50,000 weekly prize on a 50-cent ticket with more frequent drawings to keep public interest high. Still, the New Jersey lottery did not produce the revenue its supporters had claimed during the legalization campaign. By 1972, a daily lottery was instituted, and a variety of instant payoff features plus increased top prizes have followed in swift succession.[12]

Other northeastern states followed the lead and instituted lotteries of their own. James E. Ritchie of the CRNPTG speculated that what occurred was a "domino effect" as states adopted lotteries only because their neighbors had, regardless of results.[13]

Until 1975, lottery directors had a ready scapegoat for their lotteries' poor performance: the federal government. Federal law still prohibited use of the mails for gambling purposes, and the FCC still forbade radio and television advertising. Pressure from states with lotteries persuaded the 93rd Congress to rescind these prohibitions at the end of 1975. Despite this relaxation, the yield of lotteries continues to represent relatively small portions of their states' expenditures. New Jersey's lottery accounts for only 3 percent of state income. New York's lottery brings in only 1 to 3 percent of the state's education budget.[14]

Off-Track Betting

Nineteenth-century Americans bet on horse races with passion. Since Kentucky first legalized on-track (pari-mutuel) horse betting in 1906, more than thirty states have followed suit. New York was the first to legalize OTB in an attempt to ease New York City's recurrent fiscal crises.

Proponents of OTB had tried to market their idea in New York for more than twenty years before it was legalized. In the early 1960s, Mayor Robert Wagner supported the move. Wagner's appeal for OTB in New York City met with a cold response from Governor Nelson Rockefeller. New York City officials were heartened by a 1964 citywide referendum that approved OTB by a 3-to-1 margin. But the referendum was not binding. In 1965, one of the most outspoken proponents of OTB, John Lindsay, was elected mayor. In 1966 he too tried to gain approval from Albany, but he also met with a negative response from Governor Rockefeller.[15]

In 1969, a mayoral election year, the drive for OTB intensified as New York City rapidly approached the fiscal crisis that would finally cripple it in the early 1970s. In January, Francis Smith, president of the City Council, urged the New York state legislature to allow OTB in New York City. Smith asserted that OTB would bring in about $200 million, $100 million each for the city and the state. In the middle of February, Lindsay echoed Smith's call and the influential *New York Times* backed him up.[16]

During this intense campaign for OTB, Governor Rockefeller remained firm in his opposition despite the rhetoric about its financial promise, which became increasingly inflated.[17] When Abraham Beame announced his candidacy for city controller in late July, he made OTB the cornerstone of his fiscal plan. Beame said that a legalized OTB operation would bring in enough money to restore previous cuts in Medicaid, education, and other vital services. To Beame, OTB seemed the perfect and painless way of raising funds.[18] Lindsay, who was running for reelection on the Liberal-Independent ticket, continued to stress his belief in OTB throughout the campaign. In a letter to the governor in early September, he pleaded for a special state legislative session to solve the city's money problems and demanded that OTB be authorized immediately. In October, Lindsay stated that OTB was the "one area of local revenue that is at all meaningful."[19] In November, both Lindsay and Beame won their elections.

The 1969 election, combined with the 1964 referendum and the city's desperate need for new funds (and perhaps his impending campaign for reelection), finally brought Rockefeller around. He announced in March 1970 that, despite his opposition to OTB in principle, he would allow it because of the city's financial plight. On April 24, Rockefeller approved an OTB plan. He declared that its major purpose was to fight corruption.[20]

New York City officials moved swiftly to set up OTB, which was to be administered by a city commission. In August, a New York City politician, Howard Samuels, was appointed head of the commission and other members were named. One of Samuels' first acts was to call on the legislature to pass a constitutional amendment expanding OTB to include betting on all sports. Samuels was asking for the sensational in the hope of attaining a more modest goal: an expanded version of the original proposal. Lindsay had planned a quiet, relatively passive operation with betting limited to two races at two New York tracks per day. The betting parlors themselves were to be reminiscent of bank lobbies – staid and pristine, without television, bars, or entertainment.[21] Samuels now called for a more flamboyant approach, using numerous gimmicks to attract bettors. Included among these were OTB credit cards for telephone bettors, a law exempting OTB winnings from state income tax, betting on out-of-state races, and television coverage of local races, possibly in OTB offices.[22]

OTB was originally sold as a service to bettors who could not get to the track and who were already betting with bookmakers. But the restraint envisioned by its original promoters soon gave way. The passive enabling institution that would only move money from illegal bookies to government coffers took on a life force of its own. Under Samuels, OTB set out to create a new betting clientele. OTB advertising pleaded, "Start a new morning routine: coffee, doughnut, and the daily double." The original excitement over OTB's opening soon died down, and the original estimate of $200 million that had been tossed about during the OTB campaign was soon forgotten. The combined revenue of city and state is well under half that target, ten years after its inception.[23]

Despite the disappointing results, Samuels continued his push to expand OTB. During 1971 and 1972, numerous offices were opened in the New York City area, and OTB was introduced in other areas of the state. OTB officials offered many reasons for OTB's failure to take in what it "should." They blamed organized crime, the need for more offices, the need for more attractive winnings, the need for television coverage, and the need to expand betting days to include Sundays. This last request was granted in May 1973.[24]

Since OTB was not making its touted financial killing, officials like Samuels began to justify OTB's expansion by expounding on its ability to cut into organized crime in the city. This illusion was shattered in January 1974, when *The New York Times* published a synopsis of a confidential New York City police report, which estimated that OTB had led to a 62 percent increase in illegal betting. It also suggested that organized crime had grown since the inception of OTB. Paul F. Delise, chief of the Public Morals Division's Organized Crime Control Bureau, told *The New York Times*: "a climate has been created to gamble. Because it is now possible to bet legally on horses, thousands of people who never in the world would have thought of betting on football or basketball or baseball are now betting with bookies."[25]

Another policeman disparaged the security measures OTB instituted to prevent fraud: "I must have made half a dozen collars last year of big mob guys who had an OTB telephone credit card with them. The cards were under false names." Then an FBI expert on organized crime identified one major problem with legalized betting: "Since OTB has created new gamblers, do you then go into more different types of betting? . . . All it would do is make still more people gamble, and that would make even more business for bookmakers. They would find ways to make it more attractive to deal with them." The New York City police report quietly disappeared – an indication of how politically powerful OTB had become.[26]

The dynamic persists: conservative operating procedures and exuberant profit estimates are coupled, in order to secure gaming acceptance, only to have low profits justify doing away with conservative operating procedures. Bernard Rome, who was head of OTB under Mayor Edward Koch, suggested that OTB could live up to its promise: "With live TV and with restaurants in some parlors, we could provide a clubhouse environment that would see a business boom." He went on to say that "OTB would become a different, more exciting entertainment vehicle that would attract a different kind of customer – young executives, visiting business-

men, and couples out for an evening's entertainment."[27] Fiscal
shortfalls in legal gaming do not lead to its dissolution, but rather
to its expansion. And casino gambling appears to offer the richest
rewards.

Casinos

Casino games were also very popular during the nineteenth century. Images of gambling scenes are now etched into the
American mind. Western movies typically include a poker game
in a saloon or on a Mississippi riverboat. Gambling was always
available to the willing and moneyed. Although they were not
necessarily legal, these games flourished while authorities looked
the other way. Of course, as with the lotteries, public officials
were frequently paid for the dimness of their eyesight.[28]

During the last third of the nineteenth century, reformers attempted with little success to close down illegal gambling operations. Establishments in the large gambling centers, such as
Saratoga, New York, that catered to the wealthy were officially
forced to close their doors, but this only turned gamblers to more
secluded arenas of play. Few were fooled by the surface disap-
pearance of these establishments.[29]

The muckrakers of the Progressive era reported on widespread
underworld operations, including gambling and prostitution,
which fed graft into the upper levels of government. During this
period, reformers were investigating the close relationship between organized crime, gambling, and poverty. Perceptive analysts such as Lincoln Steffens reported in numerous articles and
books that corrupt public officials and criminal elements worked
hand in hand. Their proposed solution was to try to elect "good"
men to office – a solution that was for the most part an abysmal
failure. The impotence of this approach is demonstrated by the
crusade against police acquiescence to criminal operations in
New York City conducted by Charles Henry Parkhurst and Theodore Roosevelt, among others. A reform ticket won the municipal
election of 1895, launching Roosevelt's political career as police
commissioner, but it was swept out again in the next election.

The reformers learned, much to their chagrin, that police co-operation with gambling and criminal interests kept the entire system under some control. When the police were forced to try to close these operations, crime escalated. It seemed that little could be done at the state and local levels to root out corruption associated with gambling and related activities.[30]

In the early years of the twentieth century many states outlawed gambling. Nevada, for example, made gambling illegal in 1910.[31] But gambling continued to expand despite legal sanctions. The structure of illegal gambling changed with the passage of Prohibition in 1919. Speakeasies often provided games of chance as entertainment. The bootleg liquor business gave rise to new, financially powerful families and criminal groups. Many of the individuals involved quickly found investment in gambling a rewarding outlet for the earnings derived from illegal liquor sales. It has been suggested that heavy criminal involvement in casino gambling came about with the repeal of Prohibition in 1933 when there were vast sums of money "looking for action." In fact, bootleggers had already been involved in gambling for years before Prohibition ended.[32]

In the spring of 1931, Nevada legalized gambling. The immediate circumstances of the move were not unique; 1931 was one of the worst years of the Depression. Proponents of gambling in Nevada argued that legalization would bring the state a new influx of money and help reduce property taxes. But proponents faced a tough fight from women's groups throughout the state, who organized so effectively that legislators were leery of introducing a legalization bill. The obstacle was overcome by an assemblyman who submitted a bill along with the argument that legalization would help control the already-present illegal gambling business, a primary rationale for gambling advocates.[33]

Wallace Turner, in his 1965 book *Gambler's Money*, summarizes the results of legalized gambling in Nevada: "The legislature turned loose a group of professional gamblers on its people and on their guests, and then has spent the next three decades trying to control them."[34] To put it succinctly, these efforts failed. Gambling establishments were built throughout the state. Along with legalization came the notorious nightlife for which Nevada is famous. The wife of the Reno chief of police, Marion Welliver, recalled the opening days: "I don't know where they all came from. Maybe from over on the Coast. Oakland. Sacramento, maybe. San Francisco. They were the strangest sight I've ever seen. Big fat women had on cheap evening gowns – and they were wearing sneakers. You couldn't shove your way into those places . . . Some of the gambling houses opened and went broke in the same day."[35]

Even though there was support within the state of Nevada for gambling, the first decade of legalization was rather quiet. Games of chance could be found in local bars and small gambling houses. The current style of Las Vegas gambling did not emerge until the 1940s. Gangster Bugsy Siegel brought large amounts of money from organized crime into Nevada. He decided to build the luxurious Flamingo Hotel on what is now the Las Vegas strip. During World War II, black marketeers also found the Las Vegas gaming industry to be both an investment opportunity and a money laundry they could use to legitimize their cash.[36] Unfortunately for Siegel, delays in construction, escalating costs, and other problems infuriated his criminal backers. He was murdered in 1947 at the home of his mistress. But Siegel's murder did not stop the flow of criminal money into Nevada.

The close linkage of gambling in Nevada with a variety of criminal elements was revealed in the course of Senator Estes Kefauver's hearings on organized crime in the early 1950s. Practices such as skimming, hidden forms of ownership, and payoffs concealed as payments for services were brought to light. By 1954 it was clear that criminal elements were built into the gambling industry. During that year's gubernatorial campaign, the Las Vegas *Sun* initiated a private investigation into the establishment and control of casinos. This investigation revealed high levels of corruption.

In 1955, newly reelected Governor Charles Russell called for restructuring the regulations governing gambling and created a Gaming Control Board. Its efforts, along with the sale of many of the larger casinos to legitimate real-estate groups, led to the gradual elimination of criminal involvement in Nevada's gambling industry. Or so it was alleged. In 1976, the National Commission on Gambling found Las Vegas to be relatively free of underworld ties, but ruefully noted that financial transactions were so interwoven and complex that actual ownership of casinos was difficult to ascertain.[37]

Regulation of gambling in Nevada is multifaceted. Prior to the reforms of 1955, local control dominated and officials such as sheriffs were charged with enforcing gambling regulations. Since 1955, gambling has been controlled at the state level. Nevada now has three separate bodies responsible for control: the Gaming Commission, which has authority for the final approval of licenses; the Gaming Policy Committee, which advises on policy; and the Gaming Control Board, which carries out the actual enforcement of regulation. This last body is comprised of investigation, audit, tax and licensing, and securities and economic research divisions.[38] This is the administrative pattern essentially followed by New Jersey. As one professional gaming magazine points out, "New Jersey's present system was not designed on a system's basis, instead it was an attempt to improve Nevada's regulations."[39]

Historical Lessons

If legalized gambling – lotteries, OTB, casinos – is evaluated on its track record, it must be judged a limited failure. It has generated some revenue, but not in relation to other forms of taxation. But once a state has decided to legalize gambling, there is a self-generating tendency to expand when expected revenues do not materialize. Legalized gambling succeeds in extending the power of the state. When the intrinsic value of gambling as a revenue-raising activity is questioned, it is usually by reform-minded groups, not by state officials.

States undertaking to run a legalized gambling establishment or to regulate private gambling enterprises step into an area where moral guidelines are murky. A significant number of Americans, although not a majority, are opposed to gambling in principle. Even if this is set aside as an inappropriate basis for state policy-making, the moral context of the issue cannot be ignored. As the

New Jersey Gambling Commission noted in its 1973 report, when the state creates an industry that may adversely affect the social behavior of a significant number of Americans and lead to addiction in many cases, it is incumbent on the state to act with restraint and caution. But the desire to generate revenue dictates an opposite course of action.

For example, OTB in New York City was supposed to be a limited, respectable, quiet business. But once OTB was established, it quickly shucked these images in its noisy advertising campaign. The source of the problem here, and in other gambling operations that are state run or licensed, is that their status in the economy is uncertain. Do officials who run gambling establishments work for the state or for the industry? The answer is not so simple as it might appear. Once officials begin to manage a gambling operation, they frequently come to think of it as a private business that must be allowed to expand in a free marketplace. Yet the very nature of the business, as well as social policy, dictates that the state set limits for the activity. There is a fundamental tension inherent in the gambling industry whether it is state controlled or state run.

On the one hand is the need to generate as much revenue as possible. On the other is the need to keep a potentially harmful and corruptible industry under control. The tension has not been satisfactorily dealt with in the states that have legalized gambling. The problem is usually exacerbated by expanding state control of the gambling industry and the expansion of the industry itself. New Jersey's move into casino gaming both illustrates and extends these processes.

THE CASINO PASSAGE

Atlantic City's decline was all-embracing. The population decreased over 20 percent between 1960 and 1970, from 59,544 to 47,823. Available hotel rooms declined by nearly 40 percent. Levels of real estate and local luxury-tax collection as well as numbers of convention delegates were all receding during this period.[1] One critic wrote in 1970, "aside from the conventioneers, the typical Atlantic City tourist is either poor, black, elderly, or all three, and the change has depressed almost every aspect of the city's economy. Most of the fashionable stores have pulled out of the downtown area, although a brave corps of smaller merchants are defiantly resisting the trend."[2]

From 1965 to 1975, Atlantic City lost 4,500 jobs as its economy contracted on all levels. Unemployment and welfare rolls grew as deteriorating facilities failed to attract tourists. The city's housing stock was declining. The older areas had reached a dismal level of decay, with substantial tracts of abandoned buildings – a South Bronx by the seashore. The city had become a sanctuary for the elderly and for minority groups. The municipal government suffered from a chronic fiscal squeeze.

Many citizens desperately looked to the legalization of casino gambling to reverse the city's declining fortunes. Moneyed tourists and conventioneers would return. Employment would increase, government coffers would swell with new tax revenues, and the casinos would lift the resort economy out of the doldrums and into a vibrant new future.

Yet not until 1976, after failed attempts in 1970, 1973, and 1974, did Atlantic city successfully gain the right to operate legalized casino gambling. Why did the 1976 push succeed? A complex set of forces converged to bring about the approval of the 1976 referendum and Atlantic City's victory. The desire of the people of New Jersey for legal access to gaming tables played a substantial role, as did the widespread recognition of the need to aid the economies of both Atlantic City and New Jersey. Fear of crime receded as the need to raise revenues became more press-ing, despite Atlantic City's reputation for being one of the most corrupt towns in the nation. Equally significant, however, was the nature of power politics as practiced in New Jersey and, specifically, in Atlantic County. Corruption had helped to hasten Atlantic City's decline, but money and the traditions of power politics also brought casino gambling to Atlantic City. Knowledge of what old southern New Jersey politicians refer to as "the State of Atlantic," a corrupt but efficient political machine, is necessary to understand the passage of the 1976 referendum.[3]

The Atlantic City Machine

Atlantic City is the crown jewel of whatever political boss controls the party holding sway in Atlantic County, an area that includes twenty-three municipalities. The Atlantic County Republican Party dominated the area for most of the twentieth century.[4]

The Era of Nucky Johnson

Political scandal and Atlantic City are not strangers to each other. Seasonal resorts, by their very nature, are frequently tempted to push the boundaries of the law. With a questionable economy subject to the vagaries of climate, the pressure to give customers what they may want is constant. There is always the temptation to broaden the city's attraction by permitting floorshows a trifle more risqué than the law permits, by winking at prostitution, and by allowing some gaming, whether for small prizes at skeeball, slot machines, or floating crap games.

The very weakness of the seasonal economy leads even respectable members of the community to unconsciously permit or endorse evasion of the law. If convention goers complain that the town is a little dull, why not open it up? Innocuous games of chance are easily converted to ones that award cash prizes, and prostitution is, after all, the oldest profession. The local police and politicians become conditioned to the urgency of making a full year's living during the "season." When the situation becomes too flagrant for local inhabitants, a new group of leaders may come to power – but the basic psycho-economic rationale tends to prevail.

Atlantic City went through periods of outrage and reform over prostitution and gambling excesses in 1890 and 1908.[5] In 1911, the city's political boss, Louis Kinley, was sent to jail after an investigative committee concluded that he had profited from the installation of weakened underpinnings to the famed boardwalk.

From 1914 to 1941, Atlantic City was the private bailiwick of Enoch ("Nucky") Johnson. His power emanated from being both Atlantic County treasurer and secretary of the Atlantic County Republican Executive Committee – two of the highest positions of authority in southern New Jersey. Johnson's systematic abuse of power took the forms of simony, patronage, and voter fraud. He proved to be a master of corruption. No one could get a city or county position without being cleared by Nucky Johnson. He handpicked the city commissioners, county board members, and municipal and county judges. It was said that every cop on the beat owed his job to the Boss. County jury panels were selected by the sheriff, Nucky's brother, Al Johnson.[6]

Nucky's only legitimate income was the $6,000 a year he received as Atlantic County treasurer. To finance his extravagant way of life, Nucky turned to graft and political protection.[7] "No public road or building could be let without first seeing that Nucky was taken care of. Not a horse-race betting room, brothel, gambling casino, numbers banker, or petty racketeer could operate without 'cutting in' the boss. In magnitude these rackets, daily shaking down tens of thousands of citizens and visitors to the famous seashore resort, compared favorably with those of Al Capone in his prime."[8]

Nucky ran a well-oiled political machine. None of the internecine warfare that marked the Gangster Age in other American cities touched Atlantic City. For hometown racketeers, Nucky established a policy of laissez-faire; to outsiders, his policy amounted to protectionism. "In Atlantic City, if a New York or Chicago racketeer set up a casino or bordello, the local lads merely complained to the police vice squad, which drove the interlopers out of town."[9]

Nucky Johnson's criminal empire, built up over a quarter of a century, stood firm against a five-year federal assault, which cost the federal government over $200,000 and required the combined talents of eighteen agents from the Justice and Treasury departments. Scores of loan sharks, madams, and numbers bankers were herded into court and cited for contempt, but most refused to cooperate with the investigators. In the end, more than two thousand interviews were conducted with a wide assortment of individuals ranging from city commissioners to two-dollar whores. The federal agents variously threatened, cajoled, browbeat, and jailed the lower echelon to build solid cases against the "big boys."

Johnson became so unnerved by the government's efforts that he undertook jury tampering in the summer of 1940.[10] At the same time, a reform group had gained enough strength in Atlantic City that the newly elected mayor, Thomas Taggart, succeeded in closing down many of the sources of Nucky's money – the bordellos and horse parlors that Johnson had so carefully nurtured. The final straw came when Austin Clark, one of Johnson's flunkies, turned witness for the prosecution to avoid a lengthy prison sentence. His testimony was pivotal in sending Johnson to the federal penitentiary at Lewisburg, Pennsylvania, in 1941 for ten years for failing to pay taxes on a $171,000 income.[11] The same case led to the conviction of forty-six others for income-tax evasion.

The Era of Hap Farley

With Johnson's imprisonment in 1941, the way was clear for the emergence of Frank ("Hap") Farley as a powerful new force in southern New Jersey politics. His leap to the top of the Atlantic County machine began well before the cell door closed behind his discredited predecessor.

Farley, fresh out of Georgetown University Law School, became chief clerk of the law firm employed by both Nucky Johnson and Herman G. Orman, the reigning racketeer of Atlantic City. "Farley kept close to Johnson and was, by the late '30s, one of his ablest lieutenants. He had also won a seat in the State Legislature. When Johnson went to jail [his followers] fell into step behind the new boss – Frank S. Farley – and got him elected to the New Jersey State Senate as their representative from Atlantic County."[12]

For most of his political career, Farley was simultaneously the Atlantic County treasurer, chairman of the Atlantic County Republican Party, and a state senator. Thus Farley's power extended beyond city and county to the state level. His power base was a community with a form of government in which the highest offices (commissioners) were considered part-time jobs. There was no centralized budgeting or policymaking, no real accountability, and duplication of services was the rule rather than the exception.[13] Such a system could hardly be expected to mount an organized opposition.

The 1951 Kefauver committee hearings on organized crime in Atlantic City provided the first good look at the nature of Farley's regime. The investigation never uncovered sufficient evidence to bring indictments against Farley, but it did make him squirm. Like the federal government's campaign against Nucky Johnson, the Special Investigative Committee of the Senate queried the underlings of the regime hoping that they would betray their boss.

At that time, the most popular diversions along the boardwalk were bingo, bango, tango, pokerino, and other quasi-legal games of chance. The proprietors of these stalls were subject to shakedowns and protection schemes by both mobsters and law-enforcement officials. Dissatisfied with this state of affairs, certain proprietors (along with many bookies and madams) began to talk to the Senate investigators. What these small-time racketeers balked at was the constant pressure to "get up the green" for kickbacks to the Atlantic County Republican Club. Frank L. Smith, a pokerino operator, remembered that he delivered $250 to Frank Farley as part of the $1,000 license fee. Said Smith of the encounter: "He patted me on the back and told me, 'Anytime you need anything, Smitty, come to see me.' "[14] George McCallum, a horse-parlor operator, wanted to set up shop in 1947. McCallum knew exactly who was the man to see. At the end of his meeting with McCallum, Farley told him: "Okay son, go ahead, go out and make a living."[15] Farley's word was magic when it came to the rackets in Atlantic City.

Much of what was uncovered in 1951 by the Kefauver committee came from four conscientious Atlantic City police officers (known to investigators as the "Four Horsemen"). They informed the federal investigators of the widespread practice by city authorities of assessing each Atlantic City employee, including police officers, $30 annually for the Atlantic County Republican Club.[16] For their efforts at shedding some light on the affairs of Atlantic City and for raiding gambling dens against the express orders of their superiors, the policemen were summarily brought up on charges of extortion by city prosecutors. In one of the most sordid chapters in the history of Atlantic City, these men were forced to spend the next several years in court and before civil-service boards trying to clear their names and to gain reinstatement on the police force.[17] The message was very clear. Talking to investigators would only bring grief to the informant. No city employee ever openly attempted it again. When reform is bad for business, it does not survive – at least not in Atlantic City.

The Democratic Party was quick to issue statements condemning the mess in Atlantic City, charging that the "close political ties between gamblers and Republican members and personnel of the State Senate made a house cleaning necessary."[18] Yet the Kefauver hearings were quickly forgotten as Farley won reelection to the state senate by an even wider margin in the next general election.[19]

For more than two decades, Hap was the most powerful public

figure in the region and perhaps the state. The 1964 Democratic convention was held in Atlantic City only because Farley wanted it there. "Among the Jersey politicians he may have been the king of special interest legislation, much of which has been aimed at making Atlantic City a bigger, gaudier, and more successful convention town. It was Hap Farley who made possible the low toll Atlantic City Expressway, who brought about the new addition to the city's mammoth Convention Hall, and who kept Atlantic City free of the state sales tax."[20] Farley was also largely responsible for the construction of the Garden State Parkway, a project he just barely managed to get through Trenton since most knowledgeable people considered it economically unwarranted.

The Farley machine began to break down soon after the 1964 Democratic convention. Spurred on by unkind reporting in the out-of-town press, Atlantic City's only daily paper, *The Press*, took a good look at the state of affairs in its market. In May 1965, the paper ran a six-part story on the terrible condition of the city's poor, stressing the high rates of tubercular and venereal disease among them. The results of the inquiry were twofold. First, a powerful group of business and civic leaders headed by the mayor and the owner of the Steel Pier, George Hamid, banded together to force the removal of *The Press*'s editor. According to one civic leader, "the paper has a special responsibility in a community like this. We were getting terribly alarmed about the negative news that was being built up here and fed out of the city."[21] The publisher apparently agreed, and the editor was fired. The second and more lasting effect of *The Press* series was a recognition among the black community that the inequities of the Farley machine were a matter of direct concern to them.

The black community sought a change in the status quo, which culminated in a referendum drive to change the city's form of government from a commission to a mayoral one. Although the referendum was defeated (11,369 to 5,980), the drive forever weakened Farley's grip on the city.[22] His zealous forces so corrupted the voting process that some one hundred persons were indicted for fraud. One leader of the fight for change later remarked: "The GOP power under Farley spent so much money that there were people voting from parking lots, vacant houses, what have you, the voting irregularities were wide open."[23]

Early in 1969, Farley once again came under investigation, this time by New Jersey authorities examining organized crime in the state. The inquiry delved into Farley's well-known association with reputed Atlantic City mobster Herman ("Stumpy") Orman.[24] "All they want to do is blemish the name of Farley," said the senator, "and if it wasn't Orman, they would try to connect me with someone else. Despite all the power of the Federal Government," he added, "not one scintilla, not one iota of guilt has ever been proved in my thirty years of leadership. This is all the concoction of my political enemies. But the damage is irreparable."[25] Although there was insufficient material evidence for a grand jury, the investigation was politically damaging.

Atlantic County Democrats began to hammer away at Farley's use of voter fraud to control county politics. In the spring of 1969, they successfully petitioned the New Jersey Board of Elections to void the election of a Republican, whom Farley had backed, as county sheriff the previous November. Patrick McGahn, a leading Democrat and the attorney for the Atlantic City NAACP, charged that the Farley regime had "controlled the election turnouts by providing the Republican precinct captains with lists of eligible white voters, so they could get them to the polls while ignoring the black voters."[26] The Board of Elections also found that thousands of votes had been fraudulently cast. Besides the usual number of out-of-state and deceased voters, the board located ten votes coming from the ward for the feeble-minded in the Vineland State Home of Cumberland County.[27]

The next year, 1970, Farley's name appeared in published transcripts of wiretaps on noted East Coast Mafia leaders. Time and again, in their secret conversations, the mobsters would mention Farley as a "friend" and the "man to see" in south Jersey. One of the transcripts, recorded in 1961, mentions Farley using his connections on behalf of known criminals and gamblers to get them clubhouse seats at the Atlantic City Race Course after they had been barred from that establishment.[28] Other transcripts had mobsters remarking on the close ties between Farley and Orman.[29]

A year before he was voted out of office, Farley attempted to force through the New Jersey Senate enabling legislation for a statewide referendum that would legalize gambling in Atlantic

City. Fearing a potential backlash if he were to introduce the bill himself, Farley allowed one of his long-time political cronies, Union County Senator Frank McDermott, to act as its sponsor. Farley sat on the sidelines, feigning disinterest with statements like: "Well, if the people want it, they can have it."[30] They couldn't have it: the legislation, which would have legalized gambling without instituting any safeguards, was soundly defeated in the Senate. Farley had outfoxed himself with his low-key campaign. To sell gambling to the state legislature would require a full-fledged assault with as much hand holding, street money, and influence peddling as had been needed by any of his other pet projects.

In the campaign for state senator the following year, Farley's opponent, Joseph McGahn (brother of Patrick McGahn), made extensive use of the damaging material against Farley that had been gathered over the years by the various state and federal investigations. McGahn called for the removal of what he termed "this corrupt Republican machine."[31] The voters apparently agreed, for on November 2, 1971, fifty-nine years of uninterrupted Republican control of Atlantic County ended.

Toward Legalization

General recognition of Atlantic City's deterioration on the part of concerned citizens played a major role in Farley's downfall. His defeat did not solve the problems he helped create; the legalization of gambling was intended to do that. The movers and shakers, the shills and apologists for Atlantic City, now engaged themselves in a definite if formidable task. They would attempt to legitimate in the public conscience gambling in general and casinos in particular.

Legalization of gaming was extolled as a boon to tourism, which would help both local and state economies. Even though the New Jersey lottery enjoyed a limited success, the state's fiscal problems were pressing, and revenue would be an added bonus. Supporters ardently declared that their proposal was a democratic measure designed to give the people what they wanted.[32]

The debate was not unlike those elsewhere and, therefore, is worth pursuing in some detail.

The saga of the passage of casino gambling is one of differing themes that dominated the debate at one time or another and were finally brought together successfully. The issue of "painlessly" adding to the state's tax coffers was one of the major arguments. Over and over again, advocates said that legalized gambling was not primarily a revenue-raising measure, but they constantly quoted inflated figures for expected revenue. Therefore, despite proponents' protestation, the issue of casino gambling had to be viewed within the context of taxation.

The drive to legalize casinos was renewed in 1972. Governor William Cahill opposed the idea. He wanted the legislature to take fiscal responsibility and pass an income tax – an action few state politicians were willing to consider, especially in an election year. The determination to find other sources of revenue was the immediate attraction of the casino drive. Something more than the individual needs of a particular municipality was required to secure the attention and support of the state legislature. The new source of additional revenue that casinos offered was a powerful persuader. This became the primary focus of the procasino referendum forces as the issue reached the state capital. The fact that the lottery had raised around $60 million for education and state institutions was the starting point. Individuals in Trenton were projecting that legalized gambling would raise hundreds of millions. Alfred N. Beadleston, a Monmouth County assemblyman who opposed the state income tax, declared that gambling revenue would raise as much or more than such a tax. Frank X. McDermott, soon to be on a gambling study commission, thought that gambling would raise $500 million a year.[33]

Early in 1972, in an effort to study these claims, state Senator Wayne Dumont proposed setting up a commission to examine the entire issue. He believed that legalized gambling would eliminate organized crime in New Jersey. Dumont, who would chair the commission, wanted to hurry the study in order to be able to propose a referendum by June and place it before the voters in November. Clearly, slowing momentum for an income tax was a principal, though unstated, objective. The commission was made up of members who generally opposed an income tax and supported gambling.[34]

Several of the commission members, most notably William V. Musto, took it upon themselves to crusade for legalization during this "study."[35] Musto's evangelism illustrates the proponents' logic. He was convinced that the issue had to be placed before the people: they must be given the right to choose. Sweeping aside the moral arguments against gambling, he also dismissed the argument that legalized gambling would increase social and law-enforcement problems. "I don't think I could agree with anyone more than I do with you about the problems we would have in legalization of gambling," Musto told Attorney General George F. Kugler, Jr. "My question to you is this, aren't the problems greater today and haven't they been throughout this history . . . even greater because we haven't legalized gambling? . . . I think you will have to admit that the problems we have without legalization have been with us from time immemorial and they haven't gotten any better."[36]

To those who replied that trying something just because it has not been tried can result in even greater problems, Musto returned to the cause of democracy. "We recognize those problems, but we even have problems where we don't have legalization. We have problems whether it is legalized or not legalized. What we are trying to do, I hope, is to give the people what they want, not what I want or you want but give the people what they want."[37]

Fellow proponents on the commission brought up other reasons for legalized gambling in New Jersey. Assemblyman Vincent O. Pellecchia expressed a common concern when he asked Attorney General Kugler: "We were so successful in the lottery and because of the success of the lottery all of the other states are now, more or less, copying our lottery. Doesn't it concern you that the State of New York has already passed a legalized gambling bill and it will be on a general referendum in 1973 for the voters to decide upon?"[38] (It was defeated.) Pellecchia was subscribing to the "keeping up with the Joneses" theory of fiscal policy.

The major arguments during the commission hearings were

whether or not gambling would reduce organized crime and raise revenues. Judith Cambria, a director of the League of Women Voters of New Jersey and chairwoman of the Tax Reform Committee of the League, appeared before the commission. She reviewed the performance of past lotteries and suggested that the projections for casinos were greatly inflated: "We have heard estimates that if casino gambling were brought into New Jersey, it would bring in $200 million worth of revenue. However, Nevada which has 50 major casinos and 150 minor casinos only took in $54.9 million last year [1971]."[39] Some members of the commission ridiculed her factual analysis.

Cambria went on to discuss the detrimental effects of projecting inflated figures. "Citizens, believing the revenue to be enormous, cannot understand why it is not solving all our problems. They become suspicious and distrustful of government believing these mythical huge sums are either being wasted or going into someone else's pocket . . . From personal experience I have seen and other League members have seen the amazed reaction of citizens when the actual revenues from the lottery are contrasted with the total State budget or revenue needs for particular services."[40] She called for a responsible tax structure instead of specious panaceas such as gambling revenue.

Testimony ended in December 1972, and the commission report contained no surprises. It denied that revenue was a principal reason for legalization, even though the state's take would be "substantial." In a burst of realism, however, the commission noted: "Compared with the sales tax at present levels, or with an income tax at any levels which have been recently proposed, the most optimistic estimates of gambling revenue fade if not into insignificance, at least into a distant perspective. Compared with the massive levies of the current real property tax, they are trivial."[41]

Finally, the commission noted that significant social problems might result from legalized gambling, such as the creation of a class of compulsive gamblers. The state would cause the problem and then be forced to find the solution: "any State action to expand legal gambling will increase the State's moral obligation to address itself to the problems of compulsive gambling." After noting several reasons for opposing legalization, the commission recommended that the voters decide each gambling proposal separately by referendum.[42] Although the report was not published until February 1973, the commission's recommendation that casino gaming should be put up for referendum was made known as early as December 15, 1972. It was now up to the legislature to act.

A March 1973 poll conducted for the New Jersey Tourism and Development Association revealed that 56.6 percent of New Jersey citizens favored casino gambling, 29.4 percent opposed it, and 14 percent had no opinion. By April 1973, three gambling proposals were introduced in the Assembly. The first called for repeal of the antigaming provision in the New Jersey constitution; the second authorized legislation for a limited number of state-operated or state-licensed casinos; and the third allowed establishment of a state-supervised numbers game. But on April 16, all three measures were killed in the Republican caucus. Governor Cahill and Superintendent of New Jersey State Police David Kelly, both of whom stressed the likely increase in crime, were instrumental in persuading the Republicans to vote down the bills.[43]

The 1974 Referendum

The issue of casino gambling was far from dead, however. In the 1973 gubernatorial campaign, the Democratic candidate, Brendan Byrne, said that he would support gambling in Atlantic City if state and local referendums were held and if the casinos were state-run. The campaign itself did not deal significantly with the casino issue. In December 1973 Byrne, now governor-elect, said that he would propose a constitutional amendment to allow state-sponsored casino gambling if localities approved through referendums. He dismissed any talk of mob infiltration: "there's been no suggestion of mob influence in the New Jersey state lottery."[44]

The battle for the casino passage involved a contest between evil – crime and the age-old image of its link to gambling – and good – new tax revenues and the rebuilding of Atlantic City. But to attain this last goal, casino gaming would have to be limited to that locale.

Supporters of casino gambling now began to gear up for a new referendum campaign. This time the referendum was expected to pass the legislature and to be approved in the general election because proponents were describing legalized gambling as a fiscal necessity. The voters, they declared, were faced with the choice of an income tax or legalized gambling. But the governor-elect and the proponents were not in complete agreement. Byrne disliked the idea of an open-ended referendum that would allow gambling anywhere in the state. He wanted a bill that would limit casino gambling to Atlantic City. But the legislature passed a referendum proposal in the spring of 1974 that called on the voters to legalize gambling throughout the state, subject to local approval. The referendum was expected to pass easily in the November election.[45]

Significant opposition to the referendum did not emerge until September. Members of the state assembly, church groups, and prominent New Jersey officials, such as U.S. Senator Clifford Case, formed a coalition called Casinos, No Dice – A Citizens' Committee Opposed to Casino Gambling in New Jersey (or simply No Dice). No Dice decided to focus chiefly on the issue of organized crime in gambling. It expected to spend around $100,000 on its campaign, but only managed to spend $36,000.[46] The procasino groups, led by the Atlantic City-based New Jersey Tourism Council, announced that it planned to spend around $500,000 to promote casinos[47] and actually spent $576,000.[48]

But No Dice had hit upon a timely issue. The 1974 election came just after the downfall of Richard Nixon, and voters were distrustful of all established politicians and their claims. They doubted government's ability to prevent crime. Although the voices against the referendum were especially powerful during an election year marked by an unprecedented concern with political corruption, victory still seemed certain in late September. Governor Byrne countered the No Dice position by saying that organized crime had been in New Jersey for a long time and that it would not increase because of legalized gambling. A statewide poll revealed that at this point the referendum was favored by 55 percent of the voters with 42 percent against it. Supporters believed that casinos would reduce taxes, while opponents were afraid of organized crime infiltration. Surprisingly, 58 percent of those polled believed that casinos would attract crime to New Jersey, indicating that many supporters considered crime a reasonable price to pay for lower taxes.

Early in October, Attorney General William F. Hyland announced that organized crime was buying property in the Wildwood area south of Atlantic City. He refused to link the purchases to the casino issue, but the connection was easy to infer.[49] Following Hyland's announcement, U.S. Attorney for New Jersey Jonathan Goldstein asserted that casinos would provide economic aid for criminals, not for Atlantic City. He outlined the welter of law-enforcement problems that would follow legalization. Regarding Atlantic City itself, he pointed out: "For over two decades, both government officials and the business community have been involved in the all-encompassing corruption that has struck at the heart of its governmental process."

During February, Goldstein's office had convicted two past mayors, two commissioners, and four other Atlantic City officials of extortion, conspiracy, and bribery. At their trials it was established that businessmen were forced to pay 10 percent kickbacks to government officials in order to receive lucrative building contracts totaling hundreds of thousands of dollars.[50] Goldstein noted, "Now Atlantic City's governmental and business leaders who have permitted an omnipresent fabric of corruption in Atlantic City, who have allowed Atlantic City to deteriorate and have made few if any meaningful investments to rebuild that city, are those people who now want the state to entrust to it legalized gambling."[51] He then expressed his belief "that the very same interests which have allowed Atlantic City to deteriorate will be the sole financial beneficiaries of casino gambling." Goldstein labeled as myths the casino proponents' claims that legalization would merely eliminate unenforceable restrictions and that the casinos would divert money away from organized crime. Instead, he argued, casinos would create a new class of gamblers and would make law enforcement more difficult.[52]

On October 26, No Dice announced that twelve Protestant

denominations representing about 3,000 pulpits would be asked to preach against gambling. By the end of the month, both opponents and proponents sensed that the referendum was in trouble.[53] The final vote brought defeat for the proposal by a margin of almost three to two – about 1.5 million to 1 million votes. The negative vote was especially heavy in the northern suburbs, where fear of the criminal effects of casinos was strong.[54]

Why did casinos meet with defeat in 1974? The answer lies in both national and local factors. By 1974, the nation seemed exhausted. The memory of the Vietnam war was still fresh, and there was an overwhelming desire to return to some kind of normality. Voters were not ready to experiment, especially with a measure that might increase crime. Church and newspaper attacks on the proposal added to this feeling. A return to basic moral premises, a move into a period of national healing where traditional values could assert themselves, did not mesh easily with the casino proposal. The national mood of reaction against the corruption that had been revealed in the nation's highest office was also a contributing factor, highlighting local events.

With the February 1973 corruption trials, the specter of rampant crime and immorality in Atlantic City passed before the eyes of a public already reeling from the Watergate and other political scandals. When U.S. Attorney Jonathan Goldstein voiced his opposition to legalization, he cemented the link between casinos and corruption in the minds of voters. His vocal opposition was pivotal in turning the tide against the referendum. The public's negative perception of rampant corruption in Atlantic City, which the Goldstein charges reinforced, derailed any attempt by Atlantic County representatives to campaign enthusiastically for the referendum outside of the county. Many chose to play coy, as Farley had several years earlier. Their refusal to support the referendum publicly added to the confusion in the loosely directed procasino campaign.

Another symptom of nervousness on the part of casino advocates, perhaps reflecting the negative publicity surrounding the issue, was the overly cautious manner in which they collected funds. Contributions were purposely solicited from innocuous sources, that is, from those least likely to draw attention to the fundraising drive. In one case, James Cooper, the chief fund-raiser for the casino group, returned a company's money because "by reason of the past notoriety involving one of the stockholders, Mr. Herman Orman, it was determined that it was in the best interest of everyone to reject the contribution."[55] James Cooper later acknowledged that it was the "scare campaign of the opponents which forced his group to go to the people to finance his programs," so that "more than 45 percent of the total contributions were from amounts of less than $100."[56]

Not only did No Dice make use of the uneasy feelings most people had about corruption in Atlantic City; they also played on the great fear New Jersey voters had of organized crime and its ever-growing presence in the state. That fear was significantly heightened by the vague wording of the referendum. Although most people believed that Atlantic City was meant to be the sole beneficiary of legalization and casinos the only form of gambling allowed, the referendum permitted statewide gambling of all kinds. "Gambling dens in your own back yard" was the phrase used by the antigambling forces during the fall of 1974. The pro-gambling forces countered by arguing that passage of a local referendum was necessary before gambling could be introduced to any given municipality. But they had little success in stemming the tide.

Local political squabbles were also part of the reason for the defeat. The No Dice campaign was well orchestrated. High officials publicly expressed their opposition to legalization, and the proponents lacked strong spokesmen. Whereas some members of his administration spoke out against the referendum, Governor Byrne refused to actively campaign for it. Neither major political party displayed avid support for the measure. And, as a final straw, drops in lottery proceeds signaled that gambling might not after all be such an attractive alternative to other forms of taxation.

For the losers in Atlantic City, the postmortem was an especially bitter affair. Many referendum supporters were not crusading for gambling per se. They saw in legalization salvation for the city. When their battle seemed lost, they fell to attacking one another, the governor, and especially the campaign of the opposition. "They warned that the casinos would bring in mobsters," said the editor of *The Press*. "They warned of prostitutes and loan sharks and the public apparently bought their arguments."[57] Warren County Senator Wayne Dumont, an early and vocal supporter of the referendum, also thought that the opposition campaign was "completely misleading and attempted to confuse the public." He blamed the governor for "not really supporting casino gambling while at the same time giving it lip service."[58] Mayor Bradway of Atlantic City disagreed: "Casinos were defeated by an emotional issue – organized crime, and the fact that there were too many unanswered questions in the minds of the voters regarding how long casinos would be restricted to Atlantic City, whether there would be slot machines, how many, and how it would all be regulated."[59]

Atlantic City and County officials learned from the defeat. In the days and months that followed, many of them analyzed the causes of their own failure. Murray Raphel, an Atlantic County official, recognized that the campaign failed to give New Jersey voters any reason for optimism about the future of Atlantic City. He was determined that any future campaign for legalized gambling would show what was right about Atlantic City, not what was wrong: "It should point to positive events, such as the groundbreaking for the Atlantic City Hilton, and to all the good things that can follow."[60] A progambling fundraiser thought the tourism committee that had organized the campaign "had done an amateurish job," adding that "it never called on the people who could really help with the North Jersey vote – people like 'Hap' Farley."[61] Supporters of legalized gambling finally realized that they would have to develop an overall strategy. A powerful bill would have to be written, one that would ensure victory. The bill would have to answer the public's questions and overcome their fears.

With spring came a renewed effort to get casinos into Atlantic City. The proponents of legalization recognized that the election turned on the highly visible issue of crime – an issue that would dissipate as the national wounds from Watergate healed. The pressures for economic growth began to dominate public discussions. The Atlantic City casino forces began to work in Trenton to put the issue back on the ballot in the upcoming 1976 election. This time around, they felt, they could avoid the major campaign problems of 1974.

In September 1975, Charles Worthington, a former school-teacher (who later sold the site of his secondary source of income, an Atlantic City marina, for $8 million), and Steven Perskie, the new county boss, both assemblymen from Atlantic County, sponsored a bill for a new referendum. Governor Byrne announced his support. Polls in early March showed that New Jerseyans supported legalized gambling 50 percent to 38 percent against. Voter concern had shifted from crime and corruption to jobs and the economy. Backers of the referendum spoke of the alleged economic benefits to New Jersey in terms of jobs and tourists.[62] The new campaign was under way. Tax revenues as such were a cold issue. Jobs and the state economy as a whole proved to be much more potent in the arena of public opinion.

The 1976 Referendum

The move to get the referendum on the 1976 ballot began in January of that year with the introduction in the Assembly of a bill similar to the Perskie-Worthington bill, this time sponsored by Atlantic County Assemblymen Perskie and Howard Kupperman (replacing Worthington, who had become county executive of Atlantic County). The bill would enable a referendum to be placed on the 1976 ballot. If passed, the referendum would allow casinos to operate only in Atlantic City. The casinos would be run by the state, and the revenues would be used to alleviate the financial burden of the elderly and the handicapped.

An enabling bill written by Atlantic County Senator Joseph McGahn was introduced at the same time as the Perskie-Kupperman bill. McGahn's bill placed casino ownership in the hands of private entrepreneurs and designated that revenues go into the general state coffers. McGahn argued that targeting revenues to specific areas "was an emotional approach. Everybody and every municipality should benefit, not simply pinpointing special groups. I would basically like to see that whatever revenues are derived be returned to municipalities, strictly for property tax relief." McGahn dismissed state-operated casinos as "nothing more than glorified bingo parlors," with dubious chances for success. The senator insisted that it would be inappropriate to "use state tax money for the establishment of gambling casinos and to use taxpayers' money as risk-capital in a gaming venture that has no guaranteed return, as with the State Lottery."[63]

The next step was obvious: the two bills must be merged. The compromise bill specified private ownership of casinos but contained the Perskie-Kupperman provision that revenues be used to help the elderly. "In taking the two bills and putting them together we can come out as three legislators all pushing one bill in one direction," said Kupperman, who then went on to explain that "this will make us a solid, united front."[64] Perskie said that he had "some reservations about private ownership" but stressed that "at this point it is vitally important that we all be proceeding on the same path . . . Senator McGahn and I sat down and reviewed both bills, and we decided that it was more important that we both be sponsoring the same legislation. We feel that the economic survival of Atlantic City is in the balance. There is a substantial likelihood, in fact a probability that the legislature is now prepared to approve a gambling referendum."[65] The right composite with which to endorse casino gaming was beginning to jell.

The three legislators now had the task of selling the bill to their colleagues. For Perskie, the cause he was selling was Atlantic City and not gambling. Determined not to repeat the mistakes of the past, he proposed in a speech before the Atlantic County Democratic Club that the issue be made the revitalization of a city through the introduction of casino-hotels. "Last time the question was casinos-yes versus casinos-no," said Perskie. "If we in this community allow ourselves to defend casinos as an idea, we are going to lose again. We must talk about the position of Atlantic City in the state's economy. I do think we can sell Atlantic City to the people of New Jersey."[66]

At this point, a voice from Atlantic City's recent past was heard. Hap Farley advised, "All the talking in the world, all the meetings mean nothing at all unless personal contacts are made . . . Your

contacts can't control the vote, but they can be the deciding factor."[67] True to his word, Farley ended his self-imposed exile to
stump for his favorite cause – Atlantic City: "All I can say is that
with what contacts I have and what friends I have, I will do the
best I can to help." Revisiting the backrooms and corridors of
power from Atlantic City to Trenton and from Camden to Bergen
County, Farley pleaded the cause, slapping every back available:
"If you can't help us, please don't hurt us – please don't hurt
us."[68]

As the right levers of public opinion and political block building
were constructed, the tide began to turn. Cumberland County
Assemblyman James Hurley, then running for Congress, reversed himself and became an active supporter of the bill. "At a
time when the Governor is cutting out such Medicaid items as
physical therapy in hospitals," remarked Hurley, "we should look
seriously to casino gambling as a way of financing these worthwhile services." Hurley also helped to abate the fears of the
peripheral resorts along the coast, explaining "that tourists aren't
going to only spend their time and money in casinos, but will
travel around and stay in other resort areas."[69]

The powerful mayor of Camden, Angelo Errichetti, later to be
indicted in the Abscam conspiracy for selling casino approvals in
Atlantic City, gave his support to the bill. "Let's get to work!" he
exclaimed. "Let's stop talking. Let's generate enthusiasm so people will be able to say, 'I helped Atlantic City.' Let's work together
and help each other. I'm working for what's good for your community. You must work for what is good for my community. Private enterprise can do it; can help bring about a thriving community where the mayor and commissioners can work for the
people."[70] Realpolitik, backscratching, Frank Farley's politics,
were at work.

By far the greatest prize was the support of the "Farley of the
North," Bergen County Sheriff Joseph Job. Job was the most
powerful political force in the most populous county in the state,
with "a quarter of a million voters at his beck and call."[71] He did
not back the 1974 referendum because no one asked him to. But
for his "old pal" Frank Farley, he would do anything. "It would

take a lot of hard work," Job reflected, "but I believe it could be sold in Bergen County, primarily on the basis that Atlantic City people deserve the chance to recover economically. I'm for it myself because it's a better break for the people, offering a lot better odds, like 37 to 1 at roulette as compared with 1100 to 1 in the State Lottery."[72]

The selling of the idea began in earnest after the bill cleared both houses in Trenton in the early summer of 1976. The proponents of casino gambling embarked upon an effort to sharpen their campaign by building an efficient organization to engineer the final push. "We must organize the political parties," said Joseph Lazarow, the new Atlantic City mayor, "we must compile a list of every organization in the state, and then we must go to them and convince them to vote in favor of casino gambling."[73] Frank Farley stressed the need to educate the public: "traditionally, only one voter in three in New Jersey votes on a public question. We must convince them not only to vote in favor of the question, but to go in and vote on the question before they vote for the candidates."[74]

Sanford Weiner had been recommended to head the Committee to Rebuild Atlantic City (CRAC) by Paul McCloskey, the California congressman. Weiner was one of the foremost campaign strategists in California and had helped McCloskey with his last election. Weiner hit the ground running. He quickly grasped the situation in New Jersey and knew how victories were achieved: "In past campaigns, I've found that there are people who want to get involved but nobody asks them, but we intend to fully and openly ask people throughout the state who want to help us to get involved . . . This will be an extremely different campaign [from the one of 1974], there will be offices everywhere in the state."[75]

Money was never a problem for Weiner. In fact he took the job only when he was convinced that he would control a million-dollar budget. (See Table 2.) "There was $50,000 from one local hotel, $10,000 apiece from a handful of others. The only major airline serving the area chipped in with $15,000 . . . By Labor Day, the million dollar goal had been half-achieved. By Election

Day it had been exceeded."[76] By far the biggest contributor was Bahama casino operator Resorts International, which gave the committee nearly $200,000 by the time the campaign was over. It contributed $9,000 when the organization set up shop in May 1976. That June it backed a $25,000 loan to the committee. When funds to CRAC were running out late in October, Resorts International came up with an additional $105,000 contribution. In addition, it spent $100,000 on its own to campaign for legalized gambling.

Weiner earmarked $168,670 (13 percent of his budget) for "street money" to help get out the vote. The city and county organizations paid workers to canvass their districts, ring doorbells, organize voting parties, and otherwise encourage a favorable voter turnout by a more or less apathetic populace. In terms of cost per vote, this investment was a bargain. For example, 37 cents of street money was spent for each yes vote in Essex County and 18 cents in Hudson County. Most of the street money went to Camden, Essex, and Hudson Counties, ensuring a massive voter turnout in these heavily populated urban areas. "It's a political fact of life in New Jersey that you have to pay people to work on Election Day," Weiner said later. "The measure of a county leader's power is how much he pays his Election Day workers – and if you don't pay, they don't work."[77]

As in 1974, the chief spokesmen for the opposition were church leaders and law-enforcement officials who worked through No Dice. But No Dice, short of funds this time around, was unable to launch a large-scale media campaign. The pro-casino forces reported spending more than $1.3 million; the No Dice group was able to raise only $21,250. Nearly half of this modest amount was raised in contributions of $100 or less; the committee that supported casino gambling secured 90 percent of its money in sums greater than $100.

Weiner was an effective leader for the procasino forces. He delighted in keeping the opposition off balance. Throughout the 1974 campaign, the most formidable opponent had been Jonathan Goldstein. In 1976 Weiner consistently attacked him in the media, taunting: "It is a shame that the United States Attorney has used something as important as the casinos are to the future well-being of Atlantic City and New Jersey to get name recognition for himself and his ambition to run for Governor."[78] He later went further: "Mr Goldstein apparently does not care about the people of Atlantic City who are out of work, hungry and living in substandard housing."[79] With such statements, Weiner set the tone of the campaign. Goldstein would talk about the campaign's "economic smokescreens," or its "callous attempts to buy votes," and Weiner would brand him a demagogue.

The referendum itself made it possible for such tactics to be effective. For those who had balked at the specter of statewide gambling dens, the referendum restricted casinos to the already sordid streets of Atlantic City. For those who disliked the idea of the state government as a participant in the merchandising of legalized vice, the referendum stipulated private ownership. For those who worried about moral consequences, the referendum promised that it would be the aged and handicapped who would profit most from legalization.

The political climate had also changed. Memories of Watergate were fading and popular attitudes shifting. Albert Marks, Jr., of the Atlantic County Improvement Authority, summed up public feeling: "New Jersey already has organized crime." This was an accepted fact. "Nobody likes to see tainted money come in, but if it stays in the background there is no harm. It isn't good maybe. But it's better than nothing."[80] Proponents argued that if casinos would stimulate the economy, with or without criminal ties, they would be useful.

When the formal campaign opened in September, a new No Dice effort was able to offer only weak resistance. It sued to have the referendum taken off the ballot on the grounds that the constitutional requirement of a three-year period before a rejected referendum can be submitted had been ignored. On October 1, the Superior Court ruled that the proposal was valid because it was worded differently from the 1974 referendum. After this defeat, the opponents did little more than point out that proponents' ads were false and misleading. No one was surprised when the voters approved the referendum by a three to two margin on November 2.[81]

Victory by the Sea

The Commission on the Review of National Policy Toward Gambling neatly summarized the full range of arguments both for and against legalized gambling.[82]

FOR LEGALIZATION

1. As an alternative to increased taxation, it is a politically feasible way to raise revenue.
2. Recognized as a small percentage of total revenue, it still enables new programs to be established and/or existing ones to be improved.
3. It is a voluntary, neutral, and nonregressive tax.
4. It preserves state revenues that would be drawn off by other states where gambling is legal or by the underworld.
5. It cuts the cost of government by eliminating the major source of corruption and reducing law enforcement activities.
6. It provides employment and stimulates the economy of depressed areas.

AGAINST LEGALIZATION

1. Gambling revenue is insufficient to offset the cost of its administration and regulation.
2. It increases law enforcement and welfare costs.
3. It is a regressive tax because it weighs more heavily on lower income groups.
4. It competes for consumer dollars, returns little to the economy for what it takes out, and is a disincentive to industry.
5. It lowers productivity and erodes the work ethic.
6. As a form of revenue, it rises and falls on the whims of consumers, competition from other states, and general economic conditions. Its revenue raising potential is limited by a saturation point.
7. Instead of luring consumers from illegal gambling, it creates new customers.
8. It simply postpones a state or local government's need to raise sufficient revenue through taxation.

Which arguments held sway in the success of the 1976 referendum? The procasino forces had found the magic combination of incentives. No Dice was running against the elderly and against the revival of a battered, broken-down community. With the help of a 60 to 1 financial advantage, the casino proponents were able to blunt the fear of crime.

Beneath the rhetoric of persuasion and the veneer of argument, however, it was politics that made for victory. To some it was the early and close relationship of Resorts International to pivotal members of the Atlantic County power structure that made the difference. This theory is based on the fact that Resorts later hired Marvin Perskie, the uncle of Assemblyman Steven Perskie, and Patrick McGahn, brother of state Senator Joseph McGahn, and had them draft much of the casino legislation "on a fat retainer." Michael Dorman, who has written extensively on organized crime, comments: "Since the Perskies and the McGahns have been political enemies for years, Resorts was assured of the support of both major factions in Atlantic City Democratic ranks . . . For good measure, Resorts assured solidarity with local Republicans by establishing close rapport with Joseph Lazarow, the GOP lawyer who headed the committee sponsoring the casino-legalization campaign and rode that issue all the way to the Atlantic City mayor's office."[83]

Sanford Weiner thought that the victory hinged upon the tactical move that brought Joseph Job into the fold. "I would go so far as to say that we could not have won the campaign without his help," said Weiner. He felt that Sheriff Job had provided the breakthrough in the north where the victory would be won or lost: "until Job came aboard we totally lacked not only a Bergen County spokesman but a spokesman for North Jersey, and he proved to be the one person who had the kind of credibility and popularity that would help us prove that we were alive and well up north."[84] Job's power to get out the vote in his county is underscored by the fact that CRAC felt no need to give the large amounts of street money to Bergen that were granted to other county machines.

These two theories are but outward manifestations of a more probable reason for the success of the second push. Resorts International had understood this deeper reason when it entered the campaign early on and quickly recruited Atlantic City officials. That corporation was simply following the time-honored traditions of Atlantic City politics, traditions that the politicians themselves may have forgotten. Nucky Johnson knew how to use friends. Hap Farley got things done. Yet those who followed these two into power proved to be rank amateurs. The first referendum was rejected by the voters because of a failure in the political will of its proponents. They were slow to follow through with the issue and content to leave others to fight their battles. The 1974 referendum was inadequately merchandised and centered on morality instead of economic necessity. The battle pitted preacher against huckster.

Sharpened by the defeat of 1974, the leading proponents of the 1976 referendum were either professional politicians or amateurs forced by circumstances or acquaintances to take a more worldly view. "The senior-citizen plan was an ancillary issue," Perskie later admitted. "Casinos were never intended to help the seniors – they were designed expressly to aid tourism in Atlantic City."[85]

In order to sell the casino issue, much had been promised. A vision of jobs and urban rebirth had been projected and had developed political potency. But these enticements generated a demand for instant action, for getting the casinos into operation, for bringing the promised land to fruition. Much of the later history of the casinos was a measure of the gap between vision and rushed reality.

RULES AND REALITY

Shortly after the 1976 referendum, the New Jersey Assembly's State Government Committee outlined a timetable for implementation, which called for the opening of the first casino by June 1978.[1] The pressures for opening quickly began to erode the nominal checks and balances that had been formulated to make casino gaming palatable to the public. (See Table 3 for a chronology.)

On one side stood a comparatively amateur state government with few precedents to serve as guideposts, other than the realities of Nevada, which had been disavowed in the course of the referendum campaign. On the other side were politically sophisticated prospective investors, who were holding out the promise of thousands of jobs and millions in tax revenues. The state had raised the lure of an economic cornucopia; delays in filling it or, even worse, not filling it at all became politically intolerable. The dynamics of the process are instructive, not merely to students of government and economics but to other jurisdictions contemplating similar steps.

The Casino Control Act was signed on June 2, 1977, but the first meeting of the Casino Control Commission was not held until October 4. This was the result of the deliberate pace of the Byrne administration in making appointments, the difficulties in finding people who would agree to serve on the commission, and the demands of the ongoing gubernatorial campaign.

The Casino Control Commission finally named by the governor with the approval of the state legislature was typical of the modern American "representative" committee. Within the limitations of a five-person board, it represented a diversity of sectors. There was the forty-five-year-old wife of a southern Jersey county surgeon, Alice D. Corsey, who combined in her person both a female and a black member. A newspaper used a second-hand paraphrase of her own statement to a visitor to describe her qualifications: "the governor might have appointed her because he wanted a woman and black on the commission. It was certainly not because she had any interest or expertise in casinos."

The vice-chairman of the commission, Kenneth MacDonald, later to be indicted in the course of the Abscam inquiry, was the former Republican mayor of Haddonfield, an affluent suburban area not far from Camden. A one-time executive with the Esterbrook Pen Company, he had recently been the head of a Ford dealership.

Two attorneys were appointed to the commission. One was Prospero DeBona, a trial lawyer in Jersey City. His major interest in the commission was to follow the governor's lead and thereby secure a judgeship for himself. The second lawyer, the only full-time commissioner, was Joseph P. Lordi, who had served as chief trial attorney for the Attorney General's office and was Essex County prosecutor (the county in which Newark is incorporated) until his appointment to the commission. The state police gave Governor Byrne a secret report before Lordi was appointed, indicating that his long-time friend had known figures in organized crime when he was a young man in Newark. In addition, the law firm of Lordi's brother had represented the brother of a reputed north Jersey mobster, Gerardo Catena. The governor, however, expressed confidence that Lordi's previous associations did not disqualify him from the post of commission chairman.

The fifth member was Albert W. Merck, multimillionaire director and heir of the Merck pharmaceutical empire. The pattern of commission voting usually records Merck as the lone dissenter, with the other commissioners dutifully following Lordi's lead.[2]

The commissioners, unlike so many other largely honorary appointees, had to face a resourceful industry that was thriving internationally, adept in handling millions of dollars in many parts of the world; an industry whose past actions had often been illegal and which was known to have criminal associations. The growth of this industry in Atlantic City can perhaps best be compared to the reestablishment of the liquor industry after Prohibition.

The committee, which had three members who openly described themselves as "never having gambled," was given the responsibility of implementing the complex set of rules developed through a year-long process of horse trading within the state government. The nominal goals advanced for the casinos illustrates the sheer complexity of their task. The staff policy group of the governor's office believed that "the most significant consideration for planning purposes was the role of casinos in stimulating convention income, resort and entertainment industries in Atlantic City."[3] Senator Perskie, one of the original sponsors of the bill, who later did yeoman work in shaping the enabling legislation, had stated: "The end is not the casino industry. The end is the tourism, resort and convention industry of Atlantic City in particular, and the State of New Jersey."[4]

An analysis of the New Jersey casino regulation program by the state of Nevada in 1979 clearly stated the differences in approach: "New Jersey does not seek to foster the gaming industry as such, but rather seeks to limit legalized casino gaming to major hotel facilities in Atlantic City as a unique tool for urban redevelopment – in contrast, Nevada recognizes that the gaming industry as a whole is vitally important to its economy."[5]

Crime was to be kept out, the Mafia was not welcome, and virtue was to reign. Gambling was not valued for itself but as a means to an end – the revitalization of Atlantic City.

[Casino] profitability is . . . not a direct function of a quality of gaming or environment in and around the casino. Corporate corruption, cheating, loan sharking, over extension of credit, insobriety, prostitution and a honky-tonk atmosphere are not antithetical to a desire for profit, and in the industry are occasionally viewed as legitimate societal overhead so long as they encourage, or at least do not interfere with, the vitality of the gambling market . . . The interest of the state and the success of casino gambling are not coterminous with the interests of the entrepreneur.[6]

The early proposals for the casinos have an air of sweet youthfulness in retrospect. The governor's staff policy group envisioned the target of the Casino Control Commission as the creation of an atmosphere of gracious social cheer that would enhance Atlantic City's appeal to family vacationers and the convention groups without, at the same time, becoming so expensive as to be exclusive.[7] The original proposals by the governor's office included limiting the casinos to 112 hours per week of gaming, prohibiting both the serving of alcohol at gambling tables and the tipping of dealers and other employees, and allowing credit only in the form of checks that would be deposited within two business days after drawing.[8]

Moreover, the licensing standards for casino employees as well as vendors were to be strictly enforced. Job applicants had to establish reputations of honesty and integrity based on a ten-year record of information relating to their families, habits, character, financial and business affairs, and personal and professional associates.[9] The requirements were so onerous – including fingerprinting, supplying handwriting samples, advance consent to searches and seizures of records, and authorized examination of all bank accounts – as to bring the American Civil Liberties Union out in opposition to them.[10] Casino hotel licenses in New Jersey would be for a one-year period, and, unlike Nevada, license renewal was not automatic.

The Casino Control Commission wielded enormous power over the casino complexes. Licensees were faced with a continuous threat of having investments that cost hundreds of millions of dollars converted into useless hotels, unless they secured "protection" from the vagaries of the commissioners and legislators, and from all the other possibilities of running afoul of the law. Of course being law-abiding should be protection enough, but most people are cautious and believe it doesn't pay to take chances; the pattern of taking out insurance just in case, by being sure of "friends," is well established in America. This policy of insurance and of shaping the realities of what would be done – and left undone – in Atlantic City was well under way before the first casino opened to standing-room-only crowds. Many of the state's initial restrictions were quickly dynamited.

The casinos lined up heavy legal talent, and the phrase used during the campaign for casino passage – "Not Las Vegas" – began to assume an even more hollow ring. While Playboy, long an operator of casinos in England, moved to have standards based on that system, of no alcohol, no tipping, and very limited credit as well as a mere fourteen hours of daily play, the Las Vegas pattern espoused by Resorts International carried the day. For example, the concept of an admission charge or a membership fee for the casinos was quickly dismissed under the argument by Resorts that the large capital investment New Jersey was requiring in Atlantic City demanded a lucrative profit potential, which meant open doors to all but minors and criminals.[11]

The casino industry was working to open quickly, but state administrative delays seemed unending. At the same time, the state of Florida had scheduled a referendum to authorize casino gambling, and Pennsylvania was permitted by its constitution to establish casinos with dispatch. The economic benefits that Atlantic City hoped to reap would be illusory if the casino industry established gambling centers in other locations. The governor became annoyed with the delays and insisted that something be done. The erosion of the balance between gambling and the state had begun. The themes of competition from other states and of enhancing operating profitability in Atlantic City in order to encourage new investment were the leitmotifs of the elaborate dance that followed.

The Erosion of State Power

The gap between statutory regulations and the realities of casino operation, between the nominal independence of state regulatory requirements and the functional reality of the state's partnership with the casinos, quickly emerged, with the Casino Control Commission becoming a relatively passive participant in the process. The realities of this "marriage" made a mockery of the promises of revitalization, of genuine growth in the tourist industry, and of the rebirth of Atlantic City.

The casinos were successful, for example, in molding the tax provisions. As one gubernatorial aide commented, "The formulation process for the taxation provisions was preempted, thoroughly and effectively, by the industry. They were their own patronage machine – their argument carried the day so easily that you could hardly describe it as a struggle."[12] Proposals on taxing the take from the casinos had varied substantially, ranging from Nevada's approximately 5.5 percent of gross revenues to figures as high as 20 percent. Early efforts had been made to dedicate at least part of these tax revenues to rebuilding Atlantic City. The state treasury department had urged the enactment of an excess-profits tax with part of it targeted to city development. The legislature paid little attention to the idea of an excess-profits tax; the revenue tax on the casinos' gross win was ultimately reduced to 8 percent, with all revenues devoted to statewide senior-citizen programs. A very vague and small bone thrown to community reinvestment was 2 percent of gross win after a casino's gross revenue had exceeded its cumulative investment.

The licensing of ancillary service industries also illustrates the gap between the hopes of legislation and the realities of administration. The investigatory structure was so preoccupied with the casino operator and employee licenses that detailed scrutiny of service industries, although mandated by law, simply did not take place. This stemmed both from the administrative burden shouldered by the regulatory agencies and from difficult statutory assumptions. The legislative requirements were conceived to prevent criminal infiltration into the casinos from ancillary services such as guard services, vending-machine companies, and casino training schools. On the whole, the state's regulatory apparatus failed to block organized crime's infiltration into the service sector. Ironically, in some instances the burden of being approved as a service industry has been accepted by only one or two companies in an industry, and the state's licensing procedures have created in essence a service monopoly, an unanticipated side-effect of the regulations.

No one anticipated the scale of investigation that was going to be required for casinos employing nearly 4,000 people each. The state created an administrative nightmare in bending over backwards to prevent criminal participation by casino employees. The sheer press of applicants and the staffing demands of the casinos made a farce of the requirements; their complexity led to avoidance, with state cooperation. A study by a major gaming magazine indicates that the New Jersey Division of Gaming Enforcement spends an average of forty hours investigating each dealer and other minor casino employees. By way of contrast, Nevada spends less than a quarter of that time in running its much less demanding check.[13]

An article in *Gaming Business Magazine* summarizes the requirements for New Jersey casino employees (the latter defined as anyone whose employment duties require authorized access to the casino):

1. The name, date of birth and occupation of every person with whom the applicant has resided during the past ten years.
2. Date and place of each of the applicant's marriages; the name and current address of all the applicant's present and former spouses.
3. The name, date of birth, place of birth and current addresses of each of the applicant's children "whether by marriage, adoption, or natural relationship."
4. A list of data about the applicant's parents, aunts and uncles and their spouses, brothers and sisters and their spouses, children and their spouses – which includes date of birth, current address and phone number and the names of the other's parents.
5. The same information listed in 4 above about the relatives of the applicant's present spouse.

In addition, the applicant must sign a waiver of liability, relinquishing any claim against the state "for any damages resulting from any disclosure or publication in any manner, other than a willingful, unlawful disclosure for publication, of any material or information acquired during the licensing process."[14]

Such procedures resulted in the creation of a vigorous bureaucracy to implement them. The two agencies responsible for carrying out the Casino Control Act – the Casino Control Commission and the Division of Gaming Enforcement – are supported by casino fees deposited into the Casino Control Fund. The regulatory agencies have grown substantially since their creation. Casino regulatory fees amounted to only $4 million in 1978, but they are around $30 million in 1982. While the two agencies had 154 employees in 1978, by the end of fiscal 1982 their total number of employees will climb to 925. The casino regulatory structure has become more elaborate and more expensive than anyone had anticipated when the system was being designed. By way of comparison, the state of Nevada has 1,300 gambling locations scattered throughout the state and a force of 1,975 to regulate their activity.[15]

Investigations are supposed to be far more than routine. Applicants file their forms with the Casino Control Commission, which sends them to the Division of Gaming Enforcement. A three-way check produces information for examination by a review team of investigators. Typically, nearly 70 percent of the applications are cleared to the legal department for transmittal to the Casino Control Commission, with the notation that the Division of Gaming Enforcement has no objection to the applicants being licensed. Of the remaining 30 percent, additional evidence is provided on 16 percent, which are then sent to the commission without objection. Eleven percent of the applications are sent to the commission without objection, but with a letter indicating that the commission should be aware of specific information in making its licensing judgment. Three percent of the applications are returned to the commission with the statement that the division has objections to the individual being licensed. The state's rejection rate is much lower than Nevada's, where far less investigative work is done, persuading New Jersey officials that their licensing system is a deterrent to applications by criminal elements.

Regardless of its effectiveness, the system has caused significant delays. The number of people applying to be casino employees far exceeded the number anticipated. Yet casinos have frequently been unable to get as many skilled employees as they would like. They needed, for example, to find croupiers, to hire table supervisors (pit bosses) with experience, and to fill the highly specialized and enormously responsible positions involved in handling literally millions of dollars in cash each day. Who can worry about the niceties of administrative balance when patrons are crowding in, eager to share in the action? The system became sufficiently overwhelmed that the division accepted priority lists from the casinos of individuals they would like to hire. The division then processed those applicants before people who had been waiting longer.[16]

When casino business was good, the number of license applicants soared beyond state competence; when the gaming take faltered, the issue was how to restore it. Lost in the shuffle was the old Atlantic City, whose problems were accentuated rather than alleviated by the advent of gaming.

The Temporary License

Faced with the problems of delay and powerful casino pressure to relax regulatory strictures, Attorney General John Degnan came up with three options. The first was to adhere to the statute that required full safeguards, despite the industry's unhappiness. The second was to speed up the investigation process, at an uncertain cost to the thoroughness of the process. The third was to amend the statute to permit the casinos to begin operations under a temporary license pending the completion of the full investigation.[17]

The attorney general denied that law-enforcement considerations would be compromised for economic benefit under the third option, but the head of the state police acknowledged that it involved a balancing of economic and law-enforcement concerns. Degnan urged the legislature to accept the accelerated licensing procedure on the grounds that it would preempt potential casino competition from other states, and would allow the state to demonstrate quickly to hesitant investors the success of an Atlantic City casino.[18]

The temporary-license procedure required a mechanism to deal with operating casinos if the temporary operators were denied a permanent license. The original statute had called for economic stability in the industry, and the state did not want to close a casino and put thousands out of work. To deal with this possibility, the proposed legislation mandated that temporary licenses be granted only after a set of trustees had been designated by the applicant with the permission of the Casino Control Commission.

If a casino operator conducting business under a temporary license were denied a full license, a conservator would be selected to run the casino until its ownership could be transferred to a suitable management. The Casino Control Commission endorsed the administration's plan for temporary licenses, and the legislature accepted it after some wrangling about the details of the conservatorship. On March 17, 1978, the governor signed the legislation permitting temporary licenses. This was the first of three major statutory changes in the Casino Control Act.

The temporary license procedure permitted Resorts International, certainly one of the more controversial casino operators, to open by Memorial Day, 1978, and to enjoy a near monopoly for a year. Resorts had a long chequered history, both in and out of the gaming business. A series of articles in *Barron's Financial Weekly* had questioned the integrity of its management and highlighted claims of fraud in the establishment of its Bahama casino. There were later assertions of bribery of government officials to keep it in operation. Resorts, as earlier described, had been key to the financing of the procasino campaign. Now, having purchased a hotel that with little alteration qualified as a casino, they stood at the gates – alone. If the state wanted to get into business fast, Resorts was the only choice.

The gross win of this relatively inexpensive, rehabilitated casino in its first year reached close to a quarter-billion dollars. Its success touched off a stampede of operators seeking to open their own places. Resorts, however, was able to maintain its monopoly position until July 1979. The temporary license accomplished its purpose, but at a cost to the original safeguards. Resorts was the casino later appraised by Attorney General Degnan as one that should not have received permanent licensing. "I still don't agree with the Resorts decision. I feel that the Resorts decision represented a tilt of the concept of economic development of Atlantic City, that the commission had to weigh, rather than toward crime control."[19]

Rouge et Noir, a major gaming periodical, later raised the issue, after Resorts secured its permanent license, as to whether there were "really any standards that apply to licensing in New Jersey." The commission could not license a group of convicted felons, because of regulatory prohibitions, and they would be unlikely to license any operation known to be controlled by organized crime. But investigators were unlikely to uncover any "smoking gun" evidence of the current organized crime connections of a sophisticated licensee.[20]

The action in the only legal gambling casino within three hours' drive of 50 million people was unbelievable. Resorts' net win in only two months exceeded its investment; by the end of the year it was well above anything seen in any Las Vegas hotel. The customers stood ten deep – the definition of a heavy roller was a New York City cab driver with $200 to burn. It was people's gaming at its best, or worst.

There were a number of complaints about Resorts' behavior in its casino during the early opening days. The complaints involved a number of conflicts with the Casino Control Commission's nominal rules of the game. Invariably, Resorts' defense was that they were doing such an enormous business that failures to properly count and account for cash, for example, were relatively trivial. In light of 4,000 new jobs, new tax revenue, land speculation, and enormous flows of legal payments to a variety of influential people (to say nothing of what went into bank accounts), a mere slap on the wrist was the most that could be expected.[21] Once the Pandora's box of casino expectations had been opened, it would have been a braver politician than any in New Jersey who would – or could – stand in the way.

In the spring of 1979, Governor Byrne visited Atlantic City to examine the expected urban redevelopment. On the boardwalk, the governor expressed to reporters his chagrin at the superficial renovations he saw. His aggravation was compounded by the enormous profits that, according to the newspapers, were flowing into the coffers of Resorts International.[22] Byrne's Democratic adminstration was worried about Republican reactions to these daily journalistic accounts of Resorts' huge profits. The administration feared that it would be charged with allowing unconscionable profits to casino operators because of the administration's close ties to the industry.

The governor's concern was translated into two policy actions. First, the Casino Control Commission adopted new regulations in May 1979, setting stricter requirements for renovation of existing hotels. The new rules were sufficiently strict that satisfactory renovation would be generally more expensive than new construction.

The second response to the governor's dismay was a proposal to increase the state's gross casino revenue tax. The governor believed he had been deceived by Resorts' protestations that they were helping to rebuild Atlantic City. Administration-backed legislation was introduced into the Assembly on May 3, 1979, raising the tax on gross revenues to 16 percent from 8 percent, and raising the tax on each slot machine from $200 to $1,100. Both taxes were presented as windfall measures; the new rates would apply only as long as Resorts possessed its monopoly. As additional casinos opened, the rates would decline on a sliding scale so that they would return to the 8 percent gross revenue rate, and slot-machine taxes to $500, when five casinos were open.

The casino industry resisted these rate changes with the backing of the region's banks. The executive vice-president of the First Pennsylvania Bank of Philadelphia argued that financing casinos was a difficult undertaking because of the industry's novelty, the uncertain dimensions of the market, the competition for construction services, the volatility of land prices, and the expense of the regulatory structure. Changes in statutory tax rates would severely compound these problems.[23] Two of the state's leading financiers, Robert R. Ferguson, chairman of the First National State Bank of New Jersey (later to be the lead mortgage holder of the ill-fated Del Webb Casino), and Robert Van Buren, chairman of the Midlantic Bank, testified before state legislators that the proposed tax increases were undesirable. They would not only have a chilling effect on the prospects of financing planned casino projects, but would also "do serious damage to the credibility of New Jersey as it reaches out and tries to attract new business."[24]

Resorts International argued that they should not be subjected to increased taxes simply because their business had been successful. They had taken risks to launch the industry, and they were reinvesting their profits in Atlantic City. Furthermore, their costs had increased far beyond their original estimates because of Casino Control Commission regulations on the size of the gaming bets and the level of regulatory fees.

A struggle ensued for a number of months between the State Government Committee and the casino industry on one side and the governor on the other. The committee chairman thought it unfair to change the tax rates after casino business decisions had been made. The governor would not sign any of the chairman's legislation for months, and he called in other committee members for a personal expression of his views on the matter. Eventually a compromise was struck, and in September 1979 the governor signed legislation increasing the gross revenue tax rate to 12 percent, with a sliding decline in rates contingent on the number of operating casinos.

Abscam

The third major set of statutory changes in the Casino Control Act was a product of the Federal Bureau of Investigation's Abscam project. The FBI's sting operation used an informant who posed as an Arab sheik trying to buy political influence. The first revelations of the Abscam scandal, broadcast by New York City's NBC affiliate, alleged that an extensive investigation of New Jersey's casino activities had revealed improper conduct. The following weekend, it was reported that a member of the Casino Control Commission had traveled to Long Island with a state senator, attended a meeting with purported casino developers where a bribe was offered, and failed to report the bribe. In addition, Senator Harrison Williams was said to have boasted to undercover FBI agents that he had convinced Commission Chairman Lordi to waive construction specifications that had saved a casino developer millions of dollars. Two days later, Kenneth MacDonald resigned as vice-chairman of the commission while denying any wrong-doing. (See Chapter 8.)

A sense of crisis enveloped the administration. Old aides and campaign advisers were assembled to help the governor develop a course of action. There was agreement that something dramatic had to be done, but little notion of what the administration's response should be. Finally, the attorney general appeared before the legislature on March 3, 1980, to advocate the restructuring of the Casino Control Commission. The objective of the "reform" was aptly summed up by a bank chairman, who testified in favor of changes in the regulatory structure, concluding that "we must get the New Jersey casino industry and its problems . . . off the front pages of the nation's press."[25] The administration's goal was to protect its golden calf, and the hapless Casino Control Commissioners fell victim to the drive for cosmetic reform.

The plan presented by the attorney general called for the replacement of the four part-time commission members with full-time appointees. The part-time commission, the administration stated, had become hopelessly overburdened. When pressed by a legislator to explain what commission problems would be cured by a shift from part-time to full-time status for four members, the responses of the administration were pretty lame. Delays in the licensing process were generally acknowledged to be the product of the detailed investigatory procedure of the Division of Gaming Enforcement rather than of commission deliberations.

When the attorney general contended that "the press of Commission business . . . has resulted in a drift away from comprehensive rule-making toward the handling of problems on an ad hoc, case by case basis," the commission chairman pointed out that the commission had 650 pages of rules and another 400 waiting to be approved.[26] The attorney general indicated the administration's desire to relieve the commission of much of its responsibility for the social development and economic growth of Atlantic City, which would presumably remove any temptations for commissioners to meet with potential casino operators in a nongovernmental situation.

The commissioners served their last political purpose when the governor signed amendments to the Casino Control Act on May 20, 1980. Their removal was politically expedient, but did nothing to address the issues of casino patronage and political corruption uncovered by the Abscam investigation. As part of the changes made in the wake of Abscam, the temporary-license procedure was repealed for casinos that had not already passed certain steps in the application process.[27]

The governor originally intended to retain Commissioner Lordi, a long-time friend, but he reversed his position when the chairman testified in opposition to the administration's reform bill before the legislature. Lordi's fate became a contest between the Legislative Committee and the Assembly Committee, and a compromise was reached allowing the chairman to serve for a portion of the statutory term, illustrating the shallowness of the response to Abscam.

Casino Patronage and Political Muscle

Other jurisdictions contemplating legalized casino gambling will examine the record of events in New Jersey to discover what lessons it contains for them. One element of political significance is particularly striking and merits serious consideration: the interconnections between the casino industry and politicians. In the referendum campaign for legalized gambling, for example, the casino industry paid more than $100,000 to the major Democratic Party organizations in the state, and they all subsequently supported the industry position.

Numerous lawyers with political experience were recruited by the casino industry to conduct their relations with the state government. A partial listing is impressive: David J. Goldberg, the former counsel to the governor and the senate majority and former transportation commissioner – Benihana; Henry Luther, former Byrne campaign manager and waterfront commissioner – Penthouse; Martin Greenberg, former Byrne law partner and chairman of the Senate Judiciary Committee – Golden Nugget; Arthur Sills, former attorney general – Bally; David Satz, former U.S. attorney for New Jersey – Elsinore Corporation, a partner of Playboy; Joel Sterns, former counsel to the governor – Resorts; Robert Wilentz, current chief justice – formerly represented Caesars Boardwalk Regency; James Dugan, former state Democratic chairman and chairman of the Senate Judiciary Committee – Prime Motor Inns.[28]

Is this relationship unique or simply characteristic of any large-scale enterprise that must conform to a variety of regulations? Is it perhaps the required response to the very intimacy and detail of the regulatory mesh that is involved?

A glance at the legislative index of New Jersey indicates the legislature's absorption in casino affairs. Some three years after the passage of the basic enabling legislation, a not atypical listing of current bills under consideration included nearly fifty involving casino operations.[29] There are also the administrative realities involved in dealing with the Casino Control Commission and the State Division of Gaming Enforcement. Local Atlantic City legislators bring to the attention of the state governing body matters of interest to the region's major industry – the casinos. Over and above these legislative and administrative elements are casino relationships with local government, from the policeman routing traffic, to the fire inspector, to the food inspector, and the like.

A complex set of players must be addressed in the course of any large real-estate development in an environmentally sensitive area. In developing the casinos themselves, for example, the coastal-zone environmental requirements are incredibly intricate. Even small residential real-estate developments involve no less than 85 separate clearances. The temptation to use "tips" within the classic definition (that is, to ensure promptness) is, at the very least, tempting.

Any business finds it essential to secure a buffer between its needs and those of the regulatory authorities. A broad variety of legal services is the typical mediatory mechanism. The issue in choosing a law firm, therefore, may not be merely legal competence but established political relationships. The ability to call on regulatory agencies and be listened to (or, for that matter, even having the calls returned by government bureaucrats) becomes the principal measuring stick in deciding upon a legal representative.

The extent of the casinos' political influence must be viewed in relation to the realities of the broader relationship of large-scale enterprises and governmental processes. Most large firms in all industries typically hire lawyers of substantial political clout, say former officeholders and fundraisers for political parties. The flow of lawyers in and out of the private sector from government is constant. This role of the legal profession, far from unique to New Jersey, is clearly the case on the national level. Major Washington law firms are usually delighted to contribute highly paid associates to work for candidates. The astute corporate leader buys into a law firm that already has developed relationships. The very act of paying their bills provides some measure of contribution, at a minimum, to future efforts in securing stronger institutional ties. The difference between "being politically active" and being a blatant bag man may be merely one of degree and of calendar within the electoral cycle.

The major law firms and power brokers utilized by the casinos are usually those employed by other large-scale enterprises. But the casinos put several unique stresses on this process. At the least, their large profits permit, and their vulnerability to regulatory fiat requires, enormous expenditures for "insurance." Moreover, as new players on the block whose dealings are closely examined and whose relationships are not clearly established, they bring to light levels of stress that other large players through custom have already routinized.

The high cost of building the casinos, the industry's incredibly rapid pace of development, and the rush to secure licensing accentuated not only the casinos' political needs, but also the scale of loss that "enemies" might cause. The potential penalties are not merely a slap on the wrist, as witness the withdrawal of the Perlman brothers from their controlling interest in Caesars World or Del Webb being forced out of its partnership in a new casino. Casinos may be as much victims as victimizers, continuously threatened by extortion in the guise of reform, but the temptation to use lawyers as vehicles for insurance is constant. To prevent potential problems, for example, Resorts International bought at the same time the services of two rival political groups in Atlantic City, the McGahn and the Perskie firms. When the rewards are very great, the insurance costs may seem quite trivial.

Once in business, the developer of a casino is extremely vulnerable. To cite a drastic case, constructing Bally's Park Place cost nearly $300 million (and even lesser casinos cost over $100 million). The carrying costs and cash-flow stringencies of delay in projects scheduled for completion within a single year are ponderous. In Bally's case, its interest charges averaged above 20 percent. Assuming $150 million committed at the midway point in the construction of the casino, Bally's financial carrying costs were nearly $100,000 a day. The fear of political or labor difficulties that would cause delay is evident, and pressures upon management to forestall them are equally so.

In a sense, then, even at its most innocent, casino development would have stretched the political fabric. And this is to say nothing of the lubricants of favoritism, consultants' fees, no-show jobs, wining and dining and simple payoffs, which are so easily built into the operations of an entertainment complex. Freebies and complimentaries of all kinds are part of their "legitimate" operating package.

A casino hotel differs from other businesses of similar scale because of the enormous flows of cash involved in its operation. Gulf Oil had to go abroad in order to put together a $20–$30 million slush fund. One could walk through Gulf's headquarters in Pittsburgh without being able to find – in cash – a thousandth of that figure. A major casino hotel thinks nothing of a million dollars in cash moving through the premises in the course of a quiet day. The potential and temptation for abuse are obvious.

The casino industry has hired thousands of employees, and many of these employees have come with political credentials. Legislators have contacted the Casino Control Commission on behalf of individual applicants "very frequently."[30] Moreover, the allure of painless taxation may be substantially augmented in a legislator's eye by the patronage elements built into gaming's regulatory structure. The possibilities open to a mayor or a governor to avoid civil-service restrictions by expanding reform-narrowed appointment lists to provide favors for legislators as well as others should not be underestimated in this regard; nor should the ability of the casinos to manipulate from their powerful position.

The casino industry has been able to produce top officials from some of the state's major banks to testify on their behalf both before the legislature and before the Casino Control Commission. Their constant refrain has been that casino managers are of good character and the state should assist their activities. Not coincidentally, they are representatives of institutions that might benefit from or already enjoy casino patronage. It is possible that any large new industry establishing its operations with great fanfare would exercise such influence – but this power in the hands of a traditionally suspect industry is troubling.

A Casino-State Partnership

New Jersey depends to a disturbing degree upon the casino industry's profitability to sustain the capital investment needed to rebuild Atlantic City and on the employment the industry stimulates in that region. The Casino Control Fund and the Casino Revenue Fund will together realize approximately $150 million for the state in 1982. Of this amount, $30 million will support the regulatory system of the Casino Control Commission and the Division of Gaming Enforcement, and $120 million will go to fund senior-citizen programs. But the referendum promise of targeting state taxes on the casinos to aid the elderly has become increasingly hollow. The state's disposition of its casino "take" vividly illustrates the gap between what the public thought it was voting for during the referendum and the changes that have evolved as the casinos have tightened their partnership with the state.

The gross revenue tax yielded over $117 million in 1982, which the casino referendum had earmarked for new programs for senior citizens and the disabled. In 1979, these funds were used to pay for the state's program of extra homestead tax exemptions for senior citizens. This program had been established and its funding level set *before* the inauguration of casino gambling. In 1980 and 1981, casino funds were spent to finance the homestead exemptions for senior citizens and the state's Lifeline Program, established in 1978, which makes a payment toward senior citizens' utility bills. The Lifeline Program was created independently of casino development, but its funding level was a product of casino-generated revenues.

For 1982, the governor recommended that these two well-established programs have their costs charged against casino revenues. Municipal governments have provided some tax relief for senior citizens, and the state provided regular homestead exemptions to all citizens in the state, including seniors, as part of its developing income-tax program. The ongoing expenditures of these programs for senior citizens are now charged to the Casino Revenue Fund, freeing revenue for other expenditures. (The 1982 state budget also proposed the funding of a new program from the Casino Revenue Fund that would make the traditional municipal homestead exemptions for senior citizens available to those who live in mobile homes, but this is trivial.)

Casino tax revenues were supposed to provide new benefits to the state's senior citizens, but in 1982 the only new benefit that is even arguably the result of casino tax revenues is the Lifeline payment. Some appropriations for this program, however, would have been made available even if there had been no gambling in Atlantic City. The other senior-citizen programs funded under the Casino Revenue Fund have essentially been transferred from other budgets or other entitlements. Even the elderly have ended up defrauded.

The reliability of the casino revenue source differs from that of most other taxes. Casino revenues now flow from nine gaming organizations. This concentration of control makes the state's revenues vulnerable to the decisions of a handful of people. If revenues were to stop flowing into the Control and Revenue Funds, the state would be compelled to make provision for almost 1,000 state employees and to generate over $100 million in added revenues to maintain the expenditures currently charged against the funds.

So the state is a partner in the gambling business and changes the administrative mechanisms and nominal targets of the casinos to ensure its yield. A startling example of this is the use of a declaration of emergency to change the blackjack rules. Under the heading "Four of Atlantic City's Seven Casinos Posted Losses for Five Months," *The Wall Street Journal* reported casino operations typically in the red for the first five months of 1981. The response was immediate: the Casino Control Commission issued an economic "emergency" waiver, on July 16, 1981, eliminating the "early surrender" in blackjack (a way for players to minimize their losses if they receive a poor hand).[31]

The impact of the early-surrender rule is indicated by the fact that the $22 million won in May 1981 at the blackjack tables represented about 13 percent of the total $170.3 million wagered on that game. With the rule change in July, the win percentages rose to 17.5 percent on a somewhat smaller base as some of the more professional blackjack players refused to play. It is important to note that the casinos were permitted to present the first five calendar-month figures without the very vigorous and profitable June results in order to defend the change in the blackjack rules.

By invoking a crisis, which is defined as an "imminent peril to the public health, safety or welfare," the Casino Control Commission was able to have the blackjack law changed immediately without a public hearing and publication of the change (with a thirty-day grace period for the public to comment).[32] The comic reality, however, was that the commission in its panic invoked powers that state agencies no longer had, since the legislature in the early part of the year had required the governor to certify these emergencies. Fortunately for the casinos, the governor promptly did.[33]

There seems to be little distinction between casino profitability and the state interest – most of the earlier pieties have been quietly allowed to languish. The peculiar success of the casinos in getting the legislature to adopt a progaming stance is illustrated in Table 4, which details some of the adopted or pending changes in administrative regulations.

Regulating and nourishing the casino industry have dominated official actions; the urban renewal of Atlantic City and aid to the elderly have faded in priority. Casino gambling is a cash-rich industry, and the law-enforcement problems it generates are legion. Law enforcement has been more time-consuming than anticipated. Most efforts of the state's regulatory system have been devoted to maintaining the integrity of casino operations. The difficulty of this task and the time devoted by the commission to the development of operating rules for the casinos have left little energy to oversee the complicated development issues of Atlantic City.

The major purpose of casino gambling in Atlantic City was to restore the convention and tourist trade, but there has been no locus of government responsibility to organize, coordinate, or even oversee the reconstruction. Even with all the good will in the world, the Casino Control Commission has been much more the prisoner of events than an independent instigator of positive policies. The casino tide was too strong, and the mixed motives of the power structures too heavy a burden. Press releases and verbalized indignation have been the sorry substitutes for action.

The establishment of the casino industry in the state has created a constituency eager to champion the industry's interests. Any large employer will carry influence, but the official representatives of Atlantic City have in effect become spokesmen for the casinos. Assemblymen from the area have consistently sponsored bills that would relax operating standards to meet casino preferences. These efforts are proving to be relentless.

When the state relies on a regulated industry to achieve a public purpose, the leaders of the industry are likely to be seen as the experts to consult. State officials have little information to use in making judgments about the operations of the industry, and they tend to accept the opinions of industry people whose experience is far greater. As we have seen with the development of the casino taxation provisions in New Jersey, these judgments are likely to be misleading and self-serving. State development of casino regulations forces state officials to make decisions in sectors where their judgment has not been tested. The results, for both good and ill, are reflected in the realities of jobs, municipal revitalization, and housing.

EMPLOYMENT

The biggest celebration in Atlantic City since V-J Day erupted when news of the approval of the 1976 casino referendum was announced.[1] Euphoria reigned supreme; the citizens of Atlantic City believed that their city's golden days would now return. The community, which had united (probably for the first and last time) to pass the referendum, viewed gambling as the panacea for all the city's ills. The desperation with which declining areas reach out for new economic activities is a key to understanding the lure of casinos.

The promise of increased employment played the largest part in winning endorsement for casino gaming. New Jersey looked to the example of Nevada, whose governor attributed a quarter of total employment in the state directly to the existence of gaming, with an additional 25 percent of its businesses indirectly dependent on it.[2]

Has the promise of jobs been fulfilled? On the surface, the creation of nearly 30,000 new casino-hotel jobs in five years is remarkable, especially since many other cities in New Jersey suffered significant declines during the same period. But the gain has not been without cost; nor have the casinos broadened the Atlantic City market as they did in Nevada. The job increase has been substantial, but the boom for the residents of the city has been generally disappointing.

The Employment Context

In order to evaluate both the traumas of the past and the significant, but narrow, employment gains that have occurred in Atlantic City, it is important to identify appropriate baselines. In the analysis that follows, data on Atlantic City and County, on several major older industrial cities of the state, and on New Jersey as a whole are used for purposes of comparison.

In the latter part of the 1960s, the jet age offered increased mobility to Americans seeking recreation, which led to an abrupt downturn in Atlantic City's fortunes. As shown in Table 5, in the first half of the 1960s, Atlantic City's employment growth lagged behind that of the state and surrounding county (7 percent versus 10.9 and 12.6 percent). But it certainly was much more vigorous than that of comparable older industrial cities in New Jersey.

The 1964 Democratic Convention, however, marked the end of the illusion of luxury in Atlantic City. The moans and groans of its participants were heard nationwide as delegates discovered that, while the old-fashioned facilities of an earlier era might be picturesque to the boardwalk observer, they were far from appealing to individuals accustomed to higher standards of resort life. The latter part of the decade witnessed the beginnings of significant decline for the city. It experienced an average job loss of over 1 percent a year while New Jersey as a whole was securing an employment gain of nearly 20 percent. Atlantic City had entered the ranks of urban losers.

The stagnation afflicting both national and state economies over the ensuing five years, from 1970 to 1975, had a disastrous impact on older cities, with Atlantic City finally attaining full status as an urban disaster area. In that five-year period, the city lost nearly one in eight jobs from its total employment base. Although its contracting economy did not replicate the more dismal experience of Newark or Camden, its failure occurred within the borders of a county whose suburban areas showed impressive growth.

A further barometer of economic decline in Atlantic City is the shrinkage in the volume of retailing activity. From 1972 to 1977, even without taking inflation into account, dollar sales in the central business district suffered a 12.4 percent decrease, with general merchandise or department stores (down 62 percent) and apparel stores (down 17.6 percent) particularly hard hit. The complementary growth (40.7 percent) in the Atlantic County Standard Metropolitan Statistical Area (SMSA) illustrates a phenomenon that was taking place not merely in the environs of Atlantic City but throughout the nation: the rise of the suburban shopping center over the central business district as the focal point for major consumer expenditures. The vacuum left behind in Atlantic City is further indicated by a substantial decrease in the number of retail establishments of all kinds during the same period: 879 establishments had diminished to 760 between 1972 and 1977. The acceptance of the casinos in the city was seen as a matter of urban life and death.

Analysis of Atlantic City's employment by sector highlights the limitations of its economy before the casinos. In the 1950s and 1960s, city officials pressed to diversify the employment base, but these efforts had very limited success. By the late 1960s, even those small gains evaporated; the slide in the city's economy was too powerful for local efforts to redress. (See Table 6.) From 1965 to 1970, for example, roughly half of the total jobs lost were in manufacturing. The rate of manufacturing decline was nearly equaled by finance, insurance, and real estate and exceeded by transportation.

Over the next five years (1970 to 1975), secondary levels of employment reacted sympathetically to contraction in primary activity, accentuating the overall decline. Wholesale and retail trade together lost more than a fifth of their total employment, costing the city as a whole more than 2,000 jobs. This experience was paralleled in communications and public utilities, where absolute

employment declined by 954 jobs. Moreover, a decline in contract construction employment by fully a third indicates the
diminishing level of new capital inputs into the city's physical
plant.

The Resurgence

It is within the ominous context of losing 4,500 jobs from 1965 to
1975 that the abrupt resurgence of Atlantic City's economic fortunes must be viewed. As shown in Table 7, from 1975 to 1980
total employment within the city expanded by nearly two-
thirds – over four times more rapidly than employment within the
state as a whole. This is particularly striking since all the older industrial cities in New Jersey remained in the throes of significant
decline. Newark, for example, lost one-tenth of its employment
base during the five-year period.

The rapid change in the city's economic base from 1975 to
1980 is documented not only in the total employment tabula-
tions, but also in its composition. Table 5-4 also shows the striking
variation in employment by sector. The expansive nature of the
casinos is in dramatic contrast to the relative decay and decline
of the older economic activities. The precipitous decline of manufacturing in the city accelerated as alternative employment opportunities became available. Job losses in wholesale and retail trade
have continued at a high rate. The decline in manufacturing and
trade is due in part to the increased land values. (See Chapter 7.)
Rising occupancy costs are as hard on businesses as they are on
residents.

Employment increases in transportation result from the enormous flow of traffic into the city stimulated by the casinos. The
traffic, however, has bypassed the older retail establishments.
Even the finance, insurance, and real-estate sectors have suffered
an employment decline, despite the high level of land speculation
and the flow of funds and payroll generated by the gaming
facilities.

The principal winners are those who build and work in the
casinos. The service sector, which encompasses the activities of

the casino hotels, secured a net addition of 14,771 jobs from 1975 to 1980, a gain of 156.3 percent over the base-year figure. Contract construction experienced an even greater rate of increase, with employment tripling. Table 8 shows equivalent data for 1980 and 1981, which serves to confirm the basic narrowness of casino-generated economic development. Although Atlantic City is faring much better than its urban counterparts in New Jersey, its economy is dependent upon casino employment. (Unaudited data through mid-1983 confirm these trends.)

An examination of the data by sector does not fully reveal the underlying dynamics. The overall gain within the service sector, dominated by rapid casino growth, obscures the losses in the classic boardwalk small businesses. The decimation of this "subsector" is hidden within the total statistics. Casino development of the city's boardwalk and the attendant escalation in land costs have substantially reduced the number of small businesses that once lined the walkway.

"The Bell Tolls for the Merchants," the headline read in the Atlantic City *Press* at the end of the 1979 summer:

> The sign in the window of the Grande Maison Blanche variety store – a fixture here for twenty years – tells a story repeated the length of the boardwalk, "lost our lease . . . Must vacate . . . Close out prices . . . the boardwalk of shops and stands and games . . . has died with a boom, not a whimper. Land values have soared leaving merchants clinging to short term leases. Casinos are moving in and they are moving out.[3]

The magnitude of the change brought on by casino gambling is reflected in a recent report by the executive director of the city's Chamber of Commerce, who reported that "of the 2100 businesses operating in Atlantic City in 1976 . . . only about 210 will be left by 1985."[4]

The upward swing in employment cannot be denied, despite these important negative factors. The casino impact has been so powerful that the use of even five-year intervals to report the gains masks the abrupt shift in the city's economy. Table 9 provides some insight into the phenomenon by presenting data on an annual base from 1975 to 1981. The gains accrued during a four-year period, with 1977 representing the nadir of the city's economic decline. Employment in the service sector, once again essentially the casinos, more than tripled from 1977 to 1981, with the opening of new facilities. But the decline in retailing seems to be independent of new casino activity and, as previously suggested, may even have been sustained by it. The manufacturing segment continues to dwindle, as does the financial sector. The vagaries of contract-construction employment parallel the development of casinos: employment tripled from 1978 to 1979 and then declined by a half by 1981.

Comparing employment by sector in Atlantic City with the equivalent figures for Atlantic County and New Jersey underscores the disproportionate job distribution in the city. Table 10 shows that manufacturing has assumed a declining role in New Jersey's total job base. The shrinkage in Atlantic City, however, has been much more substantial. The wholesale and retail trades have remained relatively constant in the state, accounting for something in excess of a quarter of the jobs in 1980. In Atlantic City, trade in 1980 provided little more than one job in six. The equivalent data for Atlantic County indicate a shift of functions from the city to the surrounding areas, particularly the evacuation of much of the city's retailing businesses to suburban facilities within the county.

Financial, insurance, and real-estate functions are surprisingly underrepresented in the city, with their proportional share in 1980 generally half that of the county or the state as a whole. Two-thirds of the jobs in Atlantic City in 1980 were in the service sector, far in excess of that for the state as a whole, where service jobs accounted for less than a quarter of the total. Clearly, Atlantic City's economy has become much less diversified since the casinos came on the scene. By September 1981, nearly three-quarters of the jobs in Atlantic City were in the service sector.

Direct Casino Employment

Despite the fact that the Atlantic City casinos are not open twenty-four hours a day, the volume of activity within them (as well as government-mandated staffing requirements, excessive according to casino operators) has generated an employment profile dissimilar to Nevada's. For example, in Las Vegas there are approximately 3 employees per hotel room. Current experience in Atlantic City is more on the order of 6.5 employees per room.[5] Some of the larger casino hotels have total employment levels in excess of 4,000 persons.

Management has bitterly complained that staffing is much more expensive in Atlantic City than in Las Vegas. In part, this stems from the Casino Control Commission requirements for high levels of supervision, in part from the relative paucity of municipal services available in contrast to those in Las Vegas. The casinos' high employment levels may even understate the full measure of their personnel costs. Off-duty policemen, for example, are utilized to control traffic in the city. These officers, though nominally on the city payroll, are paid for by the casinos. In 1979, the four casinos open at that time paid out approximately $1 million for this function.[6] Even with these employment levels, however, it is all too evident that economic activity generated by the casinos is largely self-contained, while the rest of the community's job base continues to shrink.

Unlike the pattern of development in Las Vegas, which evolved over a long period, Atlantic City's gaming industry burst on the scene. There was no skilled casino help and no time to let the work force develop. The residency requirements that were imposed precluded any significant out-of-state immigration (although the level of cheating on the residency requirement is still disputed). These combined to create an enormous escalation in the demand for those who had "casino potential" or who later developed appropriate skills.

The problems of securing clearance for prospective employees through the Casino Control Commission quickly mushroomed because the agency was completely unprepared for the enormous number of clearances required. Even as late as the winter of 1980, the State Division of Gaming had a backlog of 17,000 casino-employee license applications.[7] Four years after the passage of the Casino Enabling Act, the vice-chairman of the control commission cited five months as the minimum time needed to process a license.[8] The result was a tremendous level of salary inflation within the casinos.

The sudden increase in job opportunities that came with the rapid coming of the casinos was breathtaking for those who were employable and who could pass the security investigations of the Casino Control Commission. But unanticipated side-effects surfaced; the most significant was an enormous turnover of municipal workers. *The Wall Street Journal* observed the ramifications of the phenomenon under the headline, "Casino Fever Affects Nurses in Atlantic City."[9] As cocktail waitresses were rumored to be making upwards of $100 an evening, the allure of nursing at $6-$7 an hour – the local pay scale – quickly diminished. In one case, a local hospital had to close its intensive-care unit because of an abrupt loss of 10 percent of its nursing staff to the casinos.[10]

The impact was felt in other sectors of the economy as well. Casinos diverted employees not only from government agencies but also from local small businesses. Charles Worthington, the county administrator, stated the case clearly: "We have charted the turnover rate for county employees. It increased from 18 percent in 1977 to 23 percent in 1978 to over 28 percent in 1979. This trend is matched by every other employer in the area and has made it difficult for some to stay in business at profitable levels."[11] Undoubtedly, the limited growth of noncasino jobs within the community is to some degree explained by this observation: the casinos simply price other potential employers out of the labor market.

The Casino Control Commission requires the casinos to provide an elaborate fact sheet for each employee. The tabulation of these fact sheets awaits a leisure moment at the commission, and the detailed reporting schedules, along with enormous pressures on the commission to facilitate casino openings, have precluded any real analysis. We have been fortunate, however, to secure the present staffing pattern of one of the major casinos. (See Table 11.) The operation employs nearly 4,000 persons. Approximately 10 percent of the jobs are at salaries of $35,000 and over, while fully 1,300 – one out of three – fall into the $5,000 to $10,000 range. (A significant portion of the lowest-income group includes waiters and waitresses, whose incomes are understated by the pay level data presented in the table, which does not include tips.) The largest single group falls into the $10,000 to

$20,000 range, which includes dealers and other casino person-
nel, who make up half of the total. The full measure of income
derived by such individuals is also drastically understated, since
most of these individuals receive tips from gamers. While the precise scale of these tips has been rigorously debated by
casinos – and the IRS – they may well add approximately $5,000
in income to each of the participants in the tip pool.

In a community where the per capita income level in 1977, just
prior to the opening of the first casino, stood at $4,462 (as com-
pared with $6,492 for the state of New Jersey as a whole), such
levels of remuneration are not trivial.

Labor Patterns

In the course of the campaign to secure casino gaming in New
Jersey, gambling supporters made a strong commitment to affirmative action. The Casino Control Commission required detailed
casino reporting on minority employment. Table 11 shows employment shares of minorities and women at one casino. They
are the heaviest in the lower pay scales, but it is striking to see
more than token representation of these groups at the higher
levels. As a new industrial entrant, the casino industry is free of
historic commitments and therefore is able to provide significant
opportunities for those who find it very difficult to break into more
established industries.

The commission also called for some undefined measure of
affirmative action in the construction industry. With all good intentions, however, as an administrator of the program indicated,
"It was impossible to get enough contractors with minority
workers. Ultimately the Casino Control Commission diverted its
efforts into subsidizing a minority construction training institute.
By the time its product came on-stream, however, construction
had pretty much slowed down."[12]

The Casino Control Commission had spearheaded efforts to
secure more minority representation among vendors of goods
and services to the casinos. The nine casinos that were open or
expected to be in operation during the course of 1981 signed a
voluntary agreement encouraged by the then commission chair-

man, Joseph Lordi, to award 15 percent of all contracts of goods and services to minority businesses.[13]

Given the scarcity of minority enterprises of appropriate scale, there is some question of how rapidly this agreement will bear fruit. It does indicate, however, that the capacity of new enterprises, which do not have an historic network of vendor relationships, is much more flexible in providing contracts for minority businesses or equivalent newcomers.

As indicated earlier, there has been little growth in the older economic activities of Atlantic City, such as retailing and non-casino hotel industries. In certain sectors, there has even been a significant decline in employment. In terms of gross levels of jobs, though, this has been more than offset by the growth of casino hotel employment. Has this been substantially to the benefit of local residents? Or does it represent a bonus to newcomers or to relatively long-distance commuters?

Shortly after the coming of the casinos, a six-month residency requirement was passed as a condition of employment within the casino hotels; employee applications specifically stipulate this requirement. It is unclear how vigorously the requirement has been enforced. Rumors of convenience addresses and spurious antecedents are widespread.

Certainly, in the first three years of casino gambling, there was reason to question whether local residents were securing casino-based jobs. As Governor Byrne pointed out when he appointed a task force to study Atlantic City's jobless rate: "The City is booming now, yet it still has a seasonally adjusted unemployment rate of 13 percent."[14] This was at a time when the average rate of unemployment for the entire state was 7.4 percent, and high unemployment continued even after the casinos had generated an additional 13,000 jobs in the city.

If unemployment and welfare data are utilized as rough yardsticks of gaming's impact on local conditions, some measure of success is apparent in breaking the cycles of poverty and limited seasonal occupational opportunities within the area. Current data available for the city itself are imprecise, but some indication exists that, while *unemployment rates* have decreased quite sharply (and roughly match the equivalent for the state as a whole), the *number of unemployed* within the city and county has remained remarkably stable. (See Table 12.) In justice to the impact of the casinos, it should be noted that the absolute number of unemployed within the state as a whole increased in the three years from 1979 to 1981, the years upon which this judgment is made. Comparatively, therefore, Atlantic City and County are doing better, but there is some evidence of a relatively high absolute threshold of unemployment, which has not yielded to casino-related growth. As additional casinos open in the future, unemployment levels may alter significantly. But seasonality of employment still bedevils Atlantic County. The most recent data indicate a near 50 percent increase in unemployment between the third and fourth quarters of 1981.

The paucity of job opportunities over a long period, particularly for minorities in such a depressed area, has created a whole generation of residents with substantial problems in adjusting to the workplace – even with the very best of job prospects. A recent study of public housing occupants in Atlantic City indicates the poor work histories that many of them have. In addition, the detailed barriers imposed by the Casino Control Commission's clearance procedures eliminate individuals with substantial criminal records. Unquestionably, all of this accounts in part for the enormous incongruity between employment increases in the city and the relatively small decreases in the number of unemployed and of welfare recipients.[15]

Atlantic City and its environs combine high levels of long-term unemployment and high incidences of welfare dependency with reliance on a seasonal industry (tourism). In September 1970, out of a total population of 175,000, 18,000 people in Atlantic County received support under the Aid to Families with Dependent Children program. The total number of AFDC recipients peaked in 1978 at nearly 23,000. In September 1980, with six casinos operational (or nearly so), there were still 20,435 receiving aid, that is, more than 10 percent of the population.

Even when close to 20,000 new jobs were generated by the casinos, the number of adults in the AFDC program barely altered. The precasino level of September 1976 was 6,326 adults; the 1980 equivalent was 6,388. The number of adults in the

AFDC program declined in 1981 while, by way of contrast, the AFDC rolls in New Jersey as a whole grew slightly in the years from 1978 to 1981. But there were still well over 5,000 adults receiving AFDC support and a total of 17,000 welfare persons on AFDC in Atlantic County. Even ascribing the total decline of adults in AFDC to casino gaming, the calculus seems a little one-sided; 1981's nearly 30,000 casino jobs resulted in only a thousand-person decline in the number of adults on AFDC. And this is without taking into account the impact of migration out of the county as a result of the high level of forced displacement.

The only form of direct municipal welfare responsibility in Atlantic City is the General Assistance Program, which aids individuals who do not fall into any of the more significant categorical programs maintained by the county. The total number of persons receiving assistance from this program within Atlantic City itself in 1970 was 182. A peak number, 459 persons, received aid in 1977. The total shifted downward after that year, and by September 1981 (the latest period for which comparable data are available) fell to 228 persons. This is, however, relatively minor in terms of the total welfare context. The food-stamp program is a substantially more comprehensive measure of need. But it is a difficult barometer to evaluate because of such problems as the vagaries of admission standards. For the moment, there does seem to be a slight reduction of the food aid program in Atlantic County compared with the state.[16]

Elusive Secondary Benefits

The jobs created by casino development in Atlantic City have almost all been in the sectors directly associated with the casino hotels themselves. The decline in the residential housing stock has thinned out the normal service operations of the city. Although the development of new housing is eagerly anticipated, it too remains more hope than reality. Certainly, from the viewpoint of the poor in Atlantic City, the casinos have had little impact on the employment picture, at least as measured by the data on unemployment levels and welfare. The hope of overall economic revitalization has not materialized, and whether it will or not is uncertain.

The casino industry in Atlantic City is in its infancy. It may be premature to assume that the casino job boom will not spill over into other economic sectors. While this spillover may take place over time if additional casinos come in or if convention activity increases, a broadening of the job market is still only a possibility, not a fact. Perhaps time and the maturing of the surging real-estate market will provide new opportunities. In this context, it is important to realize that before the advent of gambling just about all of the national and regional retail chains had left the city. Approximately 80 to 90 percent of the total retail volume is now estimated to be generated by locally owned businesses. As large-scale vendors have departed for the suburbs, the city has lost its role as a regional retailing center. In the words of one observer, remaining merchants "do not have the resources, nor in some cases the basic merchandizing capacity," to meet the new challenge. Moreover, land speculation has driven retail rents to prohibitive levels. And with the limited availability of housing, the casino employee tends to be a suburban resident and suburban shopper.[17]

A week does not go by without revelations of plans for hotels, housing, and retail centers, but the reality tends to be much more modest than the grandiose announcements. It is very hard to separate the chaff from the wheat among the countless proposals for new in-town shopping facilities. Developers announce malls to be built on piers jutting out into the ocean for a fifth of a mile, and other equally amorphous if less imaginative proposals.

Perhaps some of these plans will take shape. So far, though, Atlantic City's gambler is intent only on the game and has no interest in shopping or other amusements. As William H. Eames, executive director of the Greater Atlantic City Chamber of Commerce indicated, the traditional summer business has been disrupted: "It's not something that I would like to talk about but we do see a switch, a lessening of the number of visitors that come to Atlantic City for the beach. The very rise in room and meal prices, parking fees as well as the loss of traditional visitor facilities in motels and older hotels, has accounted for this in part."[18] In testimony at one of the Casino Control Commission hearings, Eames stated: "We have found a trend – which I call the race track effect. A visitor to the gambling facility tends to be single-purposed, only coming to the city for gaming and generally returning the same day. They might eat a meal or two but generally they don't travel among all the shops and attractions of the city as they used to in the summer. We have not seen any great spillover effect on the retail market for those businesses that have no direct relationship with casinos."[19]

The six Atlantic City casinos that operated during January 1981 had 3,257 guest rooms with a cumulative occupancy rate of 58.6 percent – or somewhat less than 60,000 occupied-room days. During that same month, there were 372,566 daytrippers from bus tours alone.[20]

Is the prevalence of daytrippers a transient phenomenon? Or does it mark a key difference from the situation in Las Vegas, where visitors bear substantial transportation costs and will probably attempt to amortize the costs over a somewhat longer period, or until their money runs out? The distribution of casino hotel revenues in the two locations reflects this difference. Publicly owned casino operations in Nevada (with annual gaming revenues of ten million dollars or more) generate approximately 58 percent of their revenues from casino operations, 13.7 percent from food services, 10.1 percent from beverages, and over 15 percent from room accommodations.

By way of contrast, room charges in the Atlantic City casino hotels generally contribute only about a third of the revenue percentage of their Nevada counterparts; their food and beverage operations represent only half the equivalent proportion of their desert competitors. Moreover, a substantial portion of Atlantic City's casino hotel revenue comes from complimentary services. Caesars and Bally generate roughly a third of their room revenue and a half and a third, respectively, of their food and beverage revenue from "free" facilities and services for high rollers.[21]

Other comparisons are equally compelling. Hotel occupancy rates in Atlantic City stand at a very modest 55-60 percent level as against the Las Vegas threshold of over 80 percent. The two

Hilton hotels in Las Vegas, totaling 4,000 rooms, have more facilities than the cumulative total of all the casinos built in Atlantic City through 1980.

If Atlantic City were genuinely to attempt to emulate the long-distance pulling power of Las Vegas, major investments would have to be made in a revitalized convention center, substantial hotel facilities, and significant improvements in transportation networks. The spillover of economic vitality from gaming in Atlantic City is still limited. Advocates in other regions who enviously eye the economic bonanza of Nevada's gaming facilities should not assume that the benefits can be secured in one fell swoop.

The nature of the daytripping phenomenon that predominates in Atlantic City, the pattern of the casino hotel operation as a self-enclosed island (the ideal situation from the entrepreneur's point of view), and perhaps the degree of debilitation of Atlantic City prior to the casinos have done little to ease the situation. Casino production, in terms of more jobs, is far from trivial, but it falls far short of the revitalization promised the residents of the city. Is the picture much different from what follows a sudden bolstering of local employment in, say, an energy boomtown? The level of development in the economic ecology of such boomtowns is limited and often short-lived.

Would the situation be different if casinos were introduced in Miami Beach or New York's Catskills? The bulk of the new jobs, and certainly those held by local residents, in Atlantic City are much more a result of the requirement for new hotel construction than that of the casinos themselves. In Atlantic City, the physical shells for the hotels, with few exceptions, had long passed the point of rehabilitation. This is not the case in Miami Beach or in the Catskills. The call there is for casinos to enhance present facilities rather than for casino hotels to replace them; while staffing could be increased, the level of capital construction and total service-related employment would be much more limited.

Hard times make hard choices. Casino gaming has yielded substantial job growth, but it is extremely narrow in character. The Atlantic City gamer pays nearly exclusive attention to gambling; the other functions of the city's job base languish. In our judgment, this would characterize other communities that want to adopt casinos. Las Vegas has successfully broadened its appeal through the development of good convention facilities; this has yet to be achieved by Atlantic City. And indeed, if the acceptance of gaming spreads, its pulling power and potential job-rebuilding potency must falter.

FISCAL REALITIES

As communities across the nation find it more and more difficult to meet increasing operating and capital costs from relatively stagnant tax bases, the lure of "painless" new sources of revenue becomes more attractive. Politicians confronted by a voter rebellion against rising taxes find the fiscal appeal of gaming particularly strong.

Since California voters approved Proposition 13 in 1978, the movement to limit state taxes and expenditures by law has spread. In 1981, Massachusetts passed Proposition 2½, which, unlike its predecessor in California, fell upon an empty state treasury. Hull, Massachusetts, for example, is faced with an aging infrastructure and a real-property tax base limited both by decrepitude and by the new state-mandated tax limits. The fiscal problems in Hull seemed insoluble, when MGM announced that it was willing to build a $75 million casino in the area. The promise of quick relief was enormously tempting, and Hull voters said yes in 1977; the state has yet to approve.

This is just one example of what is occurring across the country. Connecticut, which does not want an income tax; Maine, which has a disproportionate welfare burden; and Illinois, which is faced with a declining industrial base – all these states are coming to a point where the revenue potential of casino gambling may look like a unique salvation.

Moreover, although the implications of the new federalism in terms of reduced transfer payments from the federal government to municipalities are still unclear, local jurisdictions and states at least feel obliged to review the possibilities of generating new taxable enterprises. Does Atlantic City show the way?

City Taxes

The major source of funds for Atlantic City's municipal government is property taxes. Additional funds come from a luxury tax and various state programs. The casinos were expected to add to the municipal government's coffers through payment of property taxes and the urban renewal they would generate.

To the occasional visitor, the mix of dilapidated buildings and abandoned lots and gleaming new structures towering against the skyline is a source of anecdote. To municipal fiscal authorities and the local taxpayer, it can be a symbol of the community's economic distress or of fiscal wealth, particularly in a community like Atlantic City, where a large amount of the community's fiscal capacities are related to property taxes.[1] (In 1980, nearly 50 percent of total revenues, and approximately 75 percent of revenues raised directly by the city, were derived from this source.)

The casinos have enormously enhanced the local revenue-raising capacity of the city. In 1982, the casinos paid more than $36 million in property taxes to city coffers. But current municipal expenditures have also grown rapidly, and the prospective costs of increasing services and investing in infrastructure to meet the stresses caused by swift casino growth raise serious questions about the fiscal windfall that legalized gambling has offered Atlantic City so far.

In New Jersey, the property tax is levied on a base determined by the municipality. The base is the *total assessed valuation*, commonly referred to as the *ratable base*.[2] All taxable property is assessed, that is, valued for taxation, by local assessors in each municipality. The sum of these formal entries on the city's tax rolls indicates the property wealth in the municipality that is subject to taxation. A pattern of change in assessed valuations over time provides a graphic representation of the shifts in the community's economy. (See Table 13.)

The pattern in the precasino era is one of attrition. In 1972, the total assessed valuation stood at $334 million; by 1978, it had declined by nearly a twelfth to $306 million. The significance of the shrinkage in taxable property wealth is accentuated by comparing the pattern in Atlantic City with statewide statistics. During the same period, taxable property wealth for the state as a whole increased from $51.4 billion in 1972 to $89.7 billion in 1978, a gain of almost 75 percent.[3]

The decrease in assessed value in Atlantic City was due, in part, to a decrease in the properties on the tax rolls. In the earlier part of the period, this was the result of demolishing structures no longer economically viable, such as the famed Traymore Hotel, a valiant art-deco remnant of Atlantic City's former glory as a summer resort; it was dynamited and cleared from its oceanfront site just before the inauguration of the casino era. In the later years, the decrease came from tearing down existing structures in preparation for the erection of casinos.

Shrinkage of assessed values in the latter period was temporary. From 1978 to 1979, the property valuation on the tax rolls more than doubled (aided by revaluation), and it increased significantly again in 1980. A comparison with the statewide pattern of taxable property wealth accentuates the magnitude of this shift. New Jersey as a whole registered a gain of 15.4 percent in taxable valuation (to $103.5 billion) between 1978 and 1980; in Atlantic City, the increase exceeded 182 percent. But even the 1980 figure merely served as a base for a near doubling by 1982 in assessed value and an increment of nearly 2½ times in equalized valuation. (Equalized valuation is synonymous with market value as determined by analysis of sales to assessment ratios.) Atlantic City's equalized property base is now higher than Newark's – a city nearly eight times more populous.

Atlantic City's per capita tax ratables compare favorably with all but a few of the most affluent suburbs in New Jersey. (These tax ratables are the total value of taxable property within the community divided by its population, or the average taxable wealth that stands behind each individual within the community.) The upswing occurred despite large-scale demolition of taxable properties by speculators interested in underlying land values and not in improving or developing the property. The local revenue-raising capacity of the city has been enormously enhanced. The increase can be attributed primarily to the casinos and secondarily to the partial reassessment of selected properties.

The landslide proportions of casino development in Atlantic City is mirrored by the property-tax assessments. (See Table 13.) In 1977, the city's total assessment on properties either then or later to be occupied by the casinos amounted to less than $27 million, or only 8.6 percent of the total assessed valuation of the city. By 1980, the casino properties were assessed at $266 million, accounting for more than 30 percent of the city's total tax base. The 1982 totals indicate an assessment of casino properties of approximately $831 million. Ramada's Tropicana alone is assessed at $133 million, while Bally's is well over the $100 million mark and the Golden Nugget is approaching that magic threshold. During the same year, some equally productive operating casinos were assessed far more modestly. The scale of these disparities raises some question about the basis for the assessments and whether they will hold.

Assessments lag behind the realities of current markets. The gap between market and assessed values can be substantial, depending upon such variables as the age of the assessments, the rate of inflation in property values, and the advent or demise of powerful market forces (such as those represented by casinos). In order to secure market-value equivalents, County Boards of Equalization in New Jersey formulate annual equalization ratios. These ratios are used to allocate county tax levies among local taxing districts.[4] Although we will use the term "market valuation," the results of applying the ratio are also known as equalized valuation and true valuation.

Atlantic City's equalization ratios and derived market-value equivalents are presented in Table 14. The ratio for 1982 indicates that, on the basis of current sales transactions, Atlantic City's assessed valuation is only 48 percent of its market value – $1.5 billion versus almost $3.2 billion. The city has gained a much strengthened and magnified tax base with which to support the community's treasury, at least in terms of taxable property wealth.

If total taxes raised are kept constant, tax rates complement the ratable base. That is, if the ratable base rises, tax rates decrease; if it falls, rates rise. But this is only the case if municipal expenditures remain constant. If they increase, the taxes to support them must also go up. The addition of the casinos, and with them the growth of taxable property within the community, has been far from painless. Municipal expenditures have risen, if not quite so swiftly as the taxable property base.

The actual tax rates levied on properties in Atlantic City, therefore, do not fully reflect the enormous escalation of taxable valuation. In Table 15, the total tax rate on assessed valuation is listed in the first column and the equalized tax rate in the second. The last three columns show how the total assessed tax rate is divided among city functions. A residential property assessed at $10,000 in 1972, which was not reassessed through 1982, would be taxed at a rate set on the basis of the adjusted ratable base. In the base year, 1972 – when the tax rate was 5.11 percent – its tax bill would have been $511. The tax would have peaked in 1977 at $795, when the tax rate soared to 7.95 percent, and subsequently would have declined to $450 by 1982.

The reduction in the amount of property tax paid on the property in the example above does not indicate a decline in the revenues raised through property taxes in the city. The tax levies equal the product of the tax rates times the total assessed valuation. Table 16 shows that the Atlantic City property-tax levy quadrupled between 1972 and 1982, despite the fact that the total property-tax rate declined. The increase in the levy was made possible by the rapid growth in assessed valuation that followed the advent of casino gambling.

Securing increased revenues from an expanding tax base does not necessarily lead to ease in dealing with changing municipal functions. The city still lacks adequate resources to provide the services required by its distressed populations or to counteract the trauma caused by a real-estate market rampant with speculation fever. A "negative feedback" effect limits the benefits attendant to a resurging property-tax base. First, the city must share the new resources with the county. Since the county tax levy is assigned to a municipality on the basis of its proportional share of the total equalized valuation in the county, the city's share increases with its tax base. Even though this new "burden" is borne principally by the new increment to the property-tax base, it does preclude the potential use of portions of the new revenue-raising capacity to the city.

Second, the new property wealth of Atlantic City leads to a direct loss of discretionary state educational aid, which is assigned in inverse proportion to the total equalized valuation per pupil in a municipality. One major index of economic well-being in a community is the state-equalized valuation per pupil. In 1976–77, Atlantic City's valuation per pupil was far below that of New Jersey and that of Atlantic County. But when casinos joined the local tax-assessment base, an abrupt reversal occurred. The estimated figures for 1982–83 show Atlantic City with almost half again that of Atlantic County and nearly triple that of the state average. The $396,876 of property wealth per pupil estimated for 1982–83 has reached the stratospheric levels usually found only in the state's most affluent suburbs. The sharp rise in the educational levy represents in part a substitution of local property-tax revenues for state-aid revenues. In effect, the state itself is a beneficiary of the city's new resources.

Reassessment

A major cause of Atlantic City's housing problem is the enormous escalation in property values. In 1977, only 4 percent of the city's

real property was represented by vacant land.[5] (See Table 17.) Small-scale residential facilities (one- to four-unit structures) constituted almost 28 percent of the tax base, apartment houses slightly under 10 percent, and commercial facilities over 58 percent. Since a uniform taxation rate is applied to all types of property in order to determine tax levies, these percentages reflect the precasino burdens of taxation borne by each component of the real-property sector. Thus in 1977, residential and apartment parcels paid approximately 37 percent of the city's property tax bill, a burden essentially reflecting historical patterns.

A vast transformation took place by 1980. Vacant land showed the greatest change. It was assessed at less than $12 million in 1977; by 1980, its total assessment approached the $150 million level. Vacant land accounted for 17.6 percent of the total assessment base in 1980, more than four times its share in 1977.

A portion of this figure represents land parcels that became vacant or had their buildings demolished between 1977 and 1980. But the major cause of the increase is speculation on a level rarely seen outside California. It also reflects the relative ease with which vacant land can be reassessed, since the problem of high rents to carry the tax burden only becomes apparent with new development.

While the residential sector's *share* of the valuation base has virtually been cut in half from 1977 to 1980, the *assessment level* increased by more than 50 percent. The same is true for assessors' appraisals of apartments, which have risen from $27 million to nearly $50 million in three years, with little new construction to account for the jump. These increases do not result from a uniform reassessment of all residential parcels, but rather from spot reassessment procedures targeted at residential facilities within casino zones and in areas subject to heavy speculation.

In the words of an analyst for the New Jersey Department of Community Affairs:

[Reassessment] essentially is done on a piecemeal basis . . . Different neighborhoods are reevaluated each year. One particular area is that bordered by Albany, Michigan, Atlantic and Pacific Avenues. As the result of reassessment in this particular neig'

borhood, properties have tripled and quadrupled in value and tax bills increased by thousands of dollars per year. As a result of this procedure, suit has been filed with the Atlantic County Board of Taxation resulting in an injunction to the City to reassess all properties within one year. At best, however, this will not be accomplished until fiscal 1983.[6]

In the meantime, small-scale property owners have been driven to sell their properties in what amounts to fire sales because of high taxes. The pattern is striking in the Inlet area, the traditional home of the city's minority groups, particularly its Hispanic citizens. In the last several months of 1980, more than 1,000 appeals were heard by the County Board of Taxation, a number of them by residents whose assessments increased by as much as 500 percent. The Atlantic County tax administrator has ordered the city to provide a more equitable assessment of properties in this area. A complete reevaluation is due to take place in 1983, but the county tax administrator has expressed his belief that something must be done to provide relief before then because the reassessment process has already led to significant abandonment.[7] The tax relief anticipated by the presence of casinos has not materialized for residents.

Complaints about current assessments are not voiced by residential property owners alone. The casinos themselves share their dissatisfaction. Appeals for tax abatement have now been filed by almost all the casinos. Resorts International, for example, is appealing its taxes back to 1978, the year the gaming facility opened. Similarly, the Boardwalk Regency, which has already won a large assessment reduction, is continuing its appeal for further relief as well as for retrospective reimbursement of excess taxation in 1979 and 1980.

The city finance commissioner noted that the community's failure to win appeals on tax abatements awarded to casino complexes and other properties was the primary reason for increasing its reserves to cover uncollected taxes from $2.8 million in 1979 to $7.3 million in 1980. He predicted the need for even further increases in the future.[8] The confusion is difficult to exaggerate. Again in the words of the city finance commissioner: "Right now there is no rhyme nor reason to the assessments."[9]

The issues of appropriate value determinations or appraisals for income-producing properties are very complex. Traditionally, the assessments of such properties are based on the costs of acquiring and improving the land and the costs of constructing the buildings added to it. In terms of this approach, the present assessments are relatively low. The construction of Bally's, for example, cost over a quarter of a billion dollars. Much of this figure represents excessive amounts paid out in the cause of speed. Should this portion of the cost be part of the assessed value? The other possible assessment procedures also have drawbacks. The discounted cost of replacement method is always controversial, while the market-data approach, which uses patterns of resales, cannot easily be applied in Atlantic City because the data on which it is based are far too limited to permit generalization.

Increasingly, however, the courts are utilizing various adaptations of the profitability of operations or the income approach to value, which looks at profits rather than the physical structure to determine assessments. Through the use of this procedure, somewhat higher levels of assessments may be defended on appeal if the casinos are profitable. But if the casinos are unsuccessful, a pattern of abatements may well follow. In essence, the community has not secured a guaranteed future tax base but is, at least to some degree, a partner with the casinos in wanting their success. If the casinos do not thrive, taxes will not be forthcoming.

The community is already preparing for its contingent liability in the success of the casinos by establishing larger reserves, but this may be just the beginning of the process.[10]

Balancing the Municipal Books

One of the mainstays of Atlantic City's nonproperty tax base had been a luxury sales tax of 5 percent on hotel rooms, restaurants, and the like. (See Table 18.) With the decline of the tourist industry, luxury-tax receipts declined by nearly $1 million from 1970 through 1977. With the introduction of gaming, receipts nearly tripled, reaching almost $8 million by 1981.

But part of the revenues from the tax have been diverted by the state to the newly reconstituted Atlantic County Improvement Authority. The actual targets of expenditure by the Authority have not yet been specified except in very general terms, which include such phrases as "operate housing projects and to redevelop property in connection therewith." But at present, there is a strong movement to divert the bulk of the collections to the proposed convention center's revitalization.

A casino, moreover, must invest 2 percent of its gross win – after it has secured a total gross profit over its cumulative investment – in land development or housing, but the casino need not make this investment within the city.[11] For the moment, only two casinos are required to make any provision for it. The investment tax credit has been spent many times verbally, but real investments are still trivial. Therefore, Atlantic City is responsible for providing a safe environment for the casinos' patrons and for providing a full range of municipal services to the casinos and their employees, while payment for these services must be offset by the property taxes levied on the gaming facilities and very few, if any, other sources.

Municipal expenditures from the 1977 precasino era to those estimated for 1980 increased by approximately $15 million to $45.4 million. The single largest increment has been for public safety; expenditures for public safety in 1977 amounted to 37.3 percent of the total budget, while they were about 43 percent in 1980. Crime rates within the city have soared, and even the current high expenditure level may not be enough to control it. Costs of general government have risen by almost $4.5 million because of inflation and the new demands made on governmental bodies. Preliminary unaudited data indicate that municipal expenditures have continued their rise, with much of the city's enhanced revenues absorbed by public safety requirements.

In addition, an underpaid civil service sector now looks for far greater rewards. The present police chief, for example, has indicated that Atlantic City's police may look forward to becoming the highest-paid uniform service in the country.[12] The contrast to government expenditures in the areas of social services is striking. Health and welfare expenditures have barely kept pace with inflation. Even more striking is an absolute dollar decline in recreation and conservation expenditures. The largess of the casinos has not led to a significant decline in poverty, nor to an increase in the services available to the poor.

The new casinos have added to the city's infrastructure problems; sewers, roads, lighting, housing, and all the physical elements of the city are in need of improvement. Although city officials feel tremendous pressures to invest in infrastructure, and to improve municipal services, expenditures by the municipality are just beginning to reflect this.[13] The shift of the luxury tax from municipal coffers to the county may be an effort by the state to ensure the availability of funds to meet these needs, but even this commitment is threatened by the belief that the city must provide a new convention center.

Atlantic City, then, finds itself increasingly dependent upon the high property-tax assessments generated by the casinos, while the very presence of the casinos has, if anything, limited supplementary sources of funds. The casinos have proved to be something less than an unalloyed blessing. They have brought in their wake substantial requirements in municipal expenditures, some of them already reflected in the city's expenditure pattern, others delayed but pressing for attention. The city's flexibility is limited.

The State

The situation is quite different from the perspective of the state. The principle state "take" is in the form of a share of the casinos' gross revenues (or win).

Initially, the state's tax on casinos was 8 percent of the gross win after adjustments for uncollectable patron checks. When Resorts International's profits were so large that they embarrassed state officials, and even led to charges of a sweetheart deal, a new bill was rushed through the legislature in September 1979. This act, which was retroactive to July 1, 1979, raised the tax rate to 12 percent for as long as only two or three licensed casinos were in operation, 10 percent when four licensed casinos were open (August 1980), and 8 percent, the current rate, when five or more were operational (November 1980).

By basing taxes on the gross win, the state avoided the problems both of assessment procedures facing the city and (with the exception of deducting credit losses) of involvement in the details of casino operations. If, for example, the state had taxed revenues after operating expenses (net revenues), or net taxable income, which is subject to the vagaries of financing, the possibilities for evasion would multiply. By tapping the flow of funds where it does, the state has escaped the bookkeeping and administrative detail that would otherwise be required.

The size of gross win in Atlantic City that New Jersey is able to tap is enormous. Resorts International by itself generated an incredible $232 million gross win in 1979, its first full year of operation. As other casinos opened, there was a descent from this height, but at a relatively moderate rate. Even in 1982, Resorts' gross win exceeded $200 million, with the other two "seasoned" casinos (Regency and Bally) generating roughly the same total. The three leading casinos by themselves secured an aggregate gross win of just over $600 million in one year.

The casinos' productivity is staggering. A gross win of $200 million involves something on the order of six or seven times that much in terms of total gaming, conceivably as much as $1.5 billion, and all of this in a 40,000-square-foot casino. On a per-square-foot basis, at least some of the more productive casinos are generating nearly $40,000 of activity per square foot per year.

While much has been made of the seasonal fluctuation in the casinos' business, excluding December (there must be some measure of diversion of excess funds from the gaming tables to Santa Claus), there is only a slight variation in revenues from month to month. This is particularly striking in light of the difficulties of getting to Atlantic City on snow-covered roads during the winter. Again, except for December, the peak month (typically July or August) is not much more than one and a half times the trough of January or November.

The total gross win revenues for all operating casinos at this writing are summarized in Table 19. From the May 1978 inception of casino gambling through 1979, gross win revenues were $459 million. The next year saw a rise of win revenues to $643

million, and in 1981 an increase of more than $457 million to
$1.1 billion. For 1982, the total soared to $1.5 billion. The total
gross win since the inception of gaming in Atlantic City through
1982 approached $3.7 billion. The state tax on gross win was
$45 million through 1979, expanded to $68.6 million in 1980,
and reached $86 million in 1981. It exceeded $117 million in
1982. The state's total take from the opening of Resorts International through the end of 1982 was over $317 million.

State revenues from gaming in 1982, in excess of $117 million,
still represent less than 2 percent of the total state budget. And the
money has gone to the state; the promise of additional aid to the
elderly, important to the passage of the casino referendum, has
joined the other broken pledges that surrounded casino acceptance.[14]

The casinos are subject to federal taxes and a variety of additional state taxes. Table 20 shows the kinds and amounts of federal, state, and local taxes paid by Caesars Boardwalk Regency.
In one year (fiscal year ending 1980), Caesars paid $3.4 million
in state corporate income tax, as well as $732,000 in slot-
machine tax and an additional $659,000 in various state sales
and use taxes. The gross-revenue tax, however, is by far the most
significant state prize, representing approximately 79 percent of
the total state tax and 83 percent of the total minus state payroll
taxes. The total amount of taxes Caesars paid to the city is not
even a tenth of the amount paid to the state. Meanwhile, the
state's contribution of funds to the city for operations or improvements related to the casinos is negligible. Whether the state will be
able to maintain this role when other states legalize gaming and
create pressures to make Atlantic City more competitive is open
to question.

The state has further benefited through the implementation of
its riparian rights in the area, which have become a major issue of
contention. The state's rights to land that was once touched by
water, whether rivers, streams, or the ocean's tides, were ignored
for years. Since the onset of casinos, however, the state has successfully renewed its claims, many of which are based on data going back more than a hundred years. The total value of these
claims is in excess of $15 million. For example, the New Jersey

Department of Environmental Protection informed MGM-Hilton officials that they would have to pay around $2.5 million to settle riparian disputes involving streams located within their 29.4-acre site. The streams in question had been filled in more than forty years before.[15]

Will casinos continue to be a completely painless fiscal triumph for the state? Are there fiscal offsets? For the moment, the state has been remarkable only in the lack of investment or succor extended to Atlantic City and its environs. While this may change in the future, for now the state treasurer's office has been delighted to collect.

There are, however, some potential problems facing the state. As funds are diverted to the casinos, the state take from other forms of gaming may fall. One expert on the competition between casinos and racetracks, Sonny Werblin, a major entertainment entrepreneur, has suggested that "the history of all racetracks vis-à-vis casinos is that the tracks go out of business very quickly."[16]

Equally troublesome is the question of whether the *gross win*, which is a *gross loss* to the gaming customers, represents money imported into the state or funds from New Jerseyans. In terms of total number of visitors, casino gambling has been essentially a local industry. For example, Resorts conducted a survey of its clients shortly after opening. It found a typical gambler in its casino to be a married New Jersey resident in his or her thirties. Fully half of the individuals surveyed were from New Jersey, with most of the rest from New York and Pennsylvania.[17] Current studies of highway and air traffic into Atlantic City confirm those findings.[18]

Assuming that these surveys are accurate (that half the gamblers are from New Jersey), then New Jersey residents must lose $450 million at the casinos for the state to secure $72 million in taxes (as it did in fiscal year 1981; this example assumes that the other $450 million was lost by nonresidents). It is not possible to determine how this money would have been used if it had not been lost at the gaming tables. A portion of it, however, would certainly have been spent on purchases subject to other state taxes. So the casino revenue tax cannot be viewed as a 100 percent net addition to the state coffers.

The state governments in New Jersey and in Nevada use the casinos and their entrepreneurs as de facto tax collectors. The farming out of taxes by using private contractors as intermediaries is not a new government practice. Historians usually view it as a weakness. Government no longer has the capacity to secure the cooperation of the citizenry in meeting the requirements of public need, so it uses as a buffer an entity that can take resources from the citizenry without invoking their wrath. The gross cost to the individual is far higher than the portion given to the governmental entity. The bulk of the receipts remains in the hands of the contractor/collector.

In the case of New Jersey, the state granted a monopoly to a particular place, thus limiting the potential competition. Machine odds were set, as were all the other rules of the game, in cooperation with the operators but without the input of the consumers (taxpayers). If the rules prove to favor the consumer at the expense of the operator and the state, the rules may be changed, as they were when card counters were found to be walking out of the casinos with their pockets bulging. Card counters are treated like tax evaders.

More important than quibbles over any given rule is the fact that the state lends its moral authority to gaming. The state sanctions and participates in a once-tainted operation. As in the case of the expansion and broadening of the lottery offerings by the state, this is far from a passive relationship. The casinos of Atlantic City are not methadone clinics for the drug-addicted, but rather have as their patrons a large number of individuals who might otherwise never have been involved in casino gaming. The long-range effects of this on the public weal may be debated, but it does represent a radical shift in orientation. In return for its sanction, both in New Jersey and in Nevada, the state gains a relatively small share of the spoils. The private entrepreneurs of the casinos secure somewhere around $2 or $3 of return for every $1 the state receives.

The situation can be compared to one in which the Internal Revenue Service had operational costs that chewed up the bulk of actual taxes collected. Even this division of the gross win may in fact overstate New Jersey's take when the state grudgingly begins to recognize that it must plow back some of its nominal profit, lest the dismal physical realities of Atlantic City overwhelm the casinos' pulling power.

The question of whether publicly owned and operated slot-machine parlors would have been more remunerative to the state than privately owned and operated casinos in terms of net tax collections was barely considered in the course of the debate about legalized gaming. Certainly, one of the most important elements in tipping the scale toward casino hotel development was that of employment. A vision of a totally revitalized community, not merely of taxes collected, was projected. In the course of the debates, as each of the several prizes – urban renewal, fiscal improvement, new jobs – was advanced, critics who questioned the magnitude of the anticipated benefit would be silenced by the claims made for the remaining positive factors. "If you don't like the tax revenues, well just look at the employment," was a common refrain. This served to condition and limit the variety of alternative approaches to taxation through gaming that were considered in New Jersey. And now, at a time of governmental fiscal stringency, the tax flow generated by the New Jersey casinos has led resource-hungry legislators across the nation to suggest similar plans.

HOUSING

All of the stresses of rapid growth in an isolated, moribund community can be seen most clearly by examining housing. Nevada was an undeveloped state when it approved legalized casino gambling. As late as 1940, for example, the total population of Nevada was 110,000; Reno, with a population of 21,317, was the largest city in the state and Las Vegas' population was 8,422. Las Vegas, however, could – and did – expand out into the desert and now has a population of more than 165,000. In contrast, Atlantic City's population in 1940 was slightly more than 64,000, and though it had shrunk by the mid-1970s to barely 40,000, there was little physical room for development because it is on a barrier island that was already fully developed when the casino gambling referendum passed. The major portion of available land in Atlantic County is subject either to the Coastal Area Facility Review Act (CAFRA) or the Pinelands Protection Act, which are designed to protect environmentally sensitive areas.[1] Therefore, vast areas of nearby open space on the mainland are closed to development. In addition, conflicting property interests in Atlantic City, as in most older urban areas, reduce the ability of local agencies to adjust services to meet new demands.

Well before the casinos came, the housing stock in Atlantic City was aging badly. Older neighborhoods were decaying, and the number of abandoned buildings was growing. As the middle class fled the city, the vacuum left behind was filled by the elderly and minority groups.

Complicating the local housing situation is a more general problem: the 1980s seem to represent an end to America's "golden housing era."[2] A fifty-year pattern of cheap housing and cheap housing finance has been shattered, and it has become increasingly difficult to provide shelter for the middle class, much less for those with modest incomes. The impact of sustained inflation, with housing costs rising well above the general inflation level, has become a national problem. Government-supported housing is no longer able to supplement the private market as it did in earlier decades. Tax-exempt bonds, for example, were once largely devoted to financing moderate-income housing by various state governments, but now they are used for a broad range of purposes, such as industrial and commercial development, hospitals, and environmental improvements. And since the market is flooded with tax-exempt offerings, interest rates on these bonds have risen to a point where they are of little help in closing the gap between limited incomes and high housing costs even when they are used for housing.

The casinos were brought to Atlantic City, in part, to help solve the housing problem. The responsibility of the casinos to help build or finance new housing is a critical question for other areas looking to gaming as a solution to this problem. New York's Far Rockaway or Long Beach, or its old borscht circuit center in Sullivan County, or Hull in Massachusetts, are all locations that have been discussed as sites for new casinos, and each has housing as poor as Atlantic City's prior to the advent of casinos. The hopes and failures of Atlantic City's housing efforts, the pressures generated by the casinos, and the ultimate results are, therefore, particularly relevant to these and other potential casino builders.

The Housing Scene

Atlantic City's population is very different from that of the United States as a whole. The pattern of housing accommodation that existed within the city reflected the population's high level of poverty, a large proportion of elderly residents, and seasonal employment. In 1979, of the 20,457 dwelling units excluding hotels, motels, and boarding houses in the city, 1,718 were vacant, and an estimated 23 percent of the housing stock was rated substandard.[3] According to Oscar Harris, the head of the Atlantic City Housing Authority and director of urban renewal: "Prior to the passage of the referendum [on gaming] the city experienced a very severe and critical housing shortage. All that casino gambling did in terms of that particular social problem was to cause it to come to the forefront, to be highlighted."[4]

The city's housing inventory reflects the level of general economic decline within a rapidly aging central city and dying resort area, exacerbated by land speculation. The number of housing units in Atlantic City decreased by more than 10 percent from 1970 to 1980. During the same period, Atlantic County's housing supply expanded by 21 percent.[5] Statistically, the Atlantic City housing supply in 1980 appears substantial, with one housing unit for every 2.32 persons (20 percent more housing units per capita than exists in the nation as a whole). However, much of the stock was held off the market for speculation or was in such bad shape that it was uninhabitable or almost so.

Although there are a few well-kept neighborhoods, most of the housing in the city is old and run-down. Single-family houses account for about a third of the inventory, two- to four-unit housing accounts for 10 percent of the stock, and apartments over stores and offices represent 3 percent. The balance is comprised of multifamily dwellings with five or more units.[6]

More than 20 percent of the occupied housing units are subsidized; there are more than 1,600 units of public housing and an additional 2,100 units of subsidized private housing. In the spring of 1980, there were only three nonsubsidized apartment buildings over 200 units in the city as a whole.[7]

Speculation

The great Atlantic City land rush began the day after the casino gambling referendum passed. Unbridled speculation produced a host of players with expectations of quick turnovers, immediate profits, and little interest in development or improvement. The resulting inflation in land values actually precluded real development. Options on property changed hands, but no new construction followed. While the land under the housing has gone up in price, the nominal improvements on the property, at best, have been forgotten and, at worst, have been viewed as a possible impediment to ease of trade – or future development. Why rehabilitate an old apartment building when the land under it could be worth literally one hundred times its residential value as a potential casino site?

The following illustrate the speculative land fever that gripped the city:

– Two local businessmen purchased a forty-six by ninety-foot lot of boardwalk property for $550,000,[8] about ten times its pre-referendum value.

– A local banker sold the 200-room LaConcha Hotel for $2 million to two Washington, D.C., builders.[9] Less than a year later the LaConcha was sold to a local real-estate broker for $5 million.[10]

– The 250-room Colton Manor Hotel was sold for $2 million to a syndicate of Baltimore doctors.[11] A little over a year later the Colton was sold for $5 million to a Cherry Hill real-estate broker.[12]

– Two years after the passage of the gambling referendum, more than $214 million in real-estate transactions was recorded in the city. According to the city's tax assessor, this represented an increase of more than 800 percent over the two years prior to the referendum.[13]

– Two years later (1979–80), total real-estate transactions in the city more than doubled again to $436 million, a 1,600 percent increase in transactions over the two-year period prior to the referendum.[14]

The major cause of the rampant speculation is the present and prospective scale of casino development. Unquestionably, Atlantic City's zoning board aggravated the overall land value and housing problem. The city's master plan specified that casinos would be allowed only in the area immediately peripheral to the boardwalk (the one exception was Harrah's area near the marina). But the zoning board allowed some changes in use designation, which encouraged speculators to believe that casinos might be permitted in a variety of locations later on.

As Philip Caton, who chaired the governor's cabinet-level housing task force, commented, "There was an anything can happen mentality. It has been difficult to focus any attention on the uses of land for housing. The Casino Hotel Association last year [1980] projected 45 casinos in Atlantic City; land prices zoomed upward."[15]

The expectation of possible zoning changes that would allow higher density in residential areas also fed the imaginations of speculators. In the words of Al Cade, senior vice-president of Caesars Boardwalk Regency, "The problem is that casinos created a market for speculators." And in Cade's estimation, "requiring the casinos to solve all of these [housing] problems is itself inflationary. When landowners and speculators know the Commission is conditioning casino licensing on housing provision, the speculators know that the casinos have an added incentive to buy; so everybody charges big prices and just sits back and waits."[16]

The city tax assessor, William Ferry, pointed out that "the $8 to $30 a square foot that people are paying for land means that they are looking for zoning changes to higher densities." But given these prices, he added, development becomes increasingly difficult: "It is expensive, you're talking about $50,000 per unit for construction, plus the land." The latter in turn is so costly that "the parking requirement alone equals $5,000 per unit." In his opinion, "most of the land is not in the hands of ultimate users; but rather you have many speculators out there."[17] Meanwhile, the tenants – shopkeepers, amusement proprietors, and renter households – face escalating rents. Higher-rent structures are caused by both the high lending rates that now seem a permanent part of the nation's financial landscape as well as the inflated re-sale prices on property. New purchasers or speculators are sad-dled with interest rates at least twice as high as those attached to precasino mortgages. These increases are passed along to tenants and lead not only to displacement but also to vacancies, because most households with the financial means to pay the new rents can buy better homes outside the city. The combination of inflated purchase prices plus the new reality of high interest rates yielded rents that sometimes are more than quadruple precasino rents.

The battle being fought over the North Inlet section of the city, long a home to blacks, Puerto Ricans, and social-security recip-ients, but now a potential site for luxury accommodations given its location within a mile or two of the casinos, brings all these elements together. The area is now largely controlled by absentee landlords who have organized to fight any development plan that does not pay them the highest possible price for their holdings. Much of the property has been stripped of buildings by a series of fires that swept the area; and many have asserted that these fires were the work of arsonists. A walk through this desolated area is much like a stroll in the South Bronx. It is urban America at its saddest.

The Atlantic City master plan designates the area as one suitable for low-density development, but the city planning board is under pressure to rezone the area for luxury high-rise units. Current land prices can only be justified by much more intensive development. Speculation and the pressures generated by it are a form of self-fulfilling prophecy: changes in use are called for to justify inflated prices, which are based upon the belief that land-use limitations will be swept away.[18]

The high level of casino employment, nearly 30,000 jobs, has accentuated the development pressures. Total employment within the city has nearly doubled since 1975. But the new job holders cannot live in a city whose housing stock has actually de-clined. While part of the failure to cope with the housing situation may be blamed on the limited competence of local and state authorities, a substantial cause of this failure is related to the issue of conflicting goals and political will.

The City for Whom?

While the terms *displacement* and *gentrification* (the forcing out of poor residents in a neighborhood by more affluent newcomers who upgrade the property) have become synonymous in most central cities, the purely anticipatory speculation that followed casino gambling to Atlantic City has produced only displacement.

Just a very few years ago, the concept of reviving middle-class occupancy in central cities was a long-term goal of urban strategists. It has had limited success in Washington's Capitol Hill, Brooklyn's Park Slope, and equivalent areas of Philadelphia and other cities. But protests by residents against displacement, either real or anticipated, have surged. The concept that occupancy creates a right of continuance infers a new form of property; that is, the right to occupy space and accommodation based not on title but rather on tenure. If gentrification were at work, Atlantic City as a *place* would at least receive some secondary benefits; for instance, consumer expenditures from the more affluent residents would support a host of retailing and ancillary service facilities that, in turn, would generate jobs and tax revenues. When displacement is not accompanied by gentrification, none of these positive results occurs.

Casino developers, land speculators, and real-estate brokers have clearly placed a strain on the supply of affordable housing in the city with resident eviction (or threat) an all too frequent byproduct. For example:

– A 1977 study undertaken by a team of Temple University law professors found a systematic effort by landlords to evict Hispanic, poor, and elderly residents from Atlantic City's Inlet section. The study contained charges that city landlords had stopped making repairs in rental housing, increased rents, issued wholesale eviction notices, and cut off essential services.[19]

– Shortly after casino developer Del Webb purchased the President Towers Apartments, its elderly residents were notified that they had less than three weeks to leave the 225-unit dwelling.[20]

– An estimated 120 elderly residents of the city's Lou-Mar Apartments received notice in April 1979 that the new owners of the

apartments would increase their rents by as much as 400 percent with their next rent payment.[21]
– About 150 senior citizens met at the Brighton Towers in
January 1981 to protest an announcement that the building
would be converted to expensive condominiums. According to
press reports, many of the senior citizens had moved to the
Brighton Towers after having been evicted from the Ritz Apartments and President Apartments.[22]
– In March 1981, plans were announced for closing the 349-bed
Madison House Nursing Home in order to convert the building
into condominiums. Most of the patients at the Madison House
have been relocated to nearby homes in south Jersey, the
Press reported.[23]

The vulnerability of the poor, who are disproportionately
represented in Atlantic City's population, accentuates the problems of displacement. With the exception of perhaps a small
group of middle-income elderly, the bulk of Atlantic City's residents prior to the casino development were there because they
had no other choice. Even among minority groups, the young
tended to leave; the old remained.

Failure to cope with the housing issue has caused significant
displacement. The Social Security Administration, for example,
has reported substantial declines in Atlantic County's senior-
citizen population. From 1974 to 1979, while the elderly population throughout the state increased by 11.5 percent (and even
more in the southern tier counties of New Jersey), it decreased by
1.6 percent in Atlantic County. In the two years from 1977 to
1979, the number of people in Atlantic City over the age of 65 receiving social-security benefits declined by 7.2 percent, from
14,874 to 13,782. The lack of housing, coupled with high prices,
is cited by the New Jersey Department of Community Affairs as
the major deterrent for such seniors.[24]

While a large percentage of the elderly population was forced
to leave Atlantic City, the figures also are a result of natural attrition and the decreasing appeal of the community to senior
citizens who might otherwise have moved there. These potential
residents moved to more hospitable areas, such as the specialized

retirement communities that have sprung up in the southern New Jersey shore counties.

Resident minority groups, however, have a much more serious problem. Other areas are far less hospitable to them than Atlantic City, which historically has had a large minority population. Thus, every housing unit lost represents real costs and often leads to displacement. The projected new housing has rent levels well over $400 a month, substantially more than twice the level that had been typical for the minority community.

Tenants of low-rent housing are viewed as momentary inconveniences rather than as long-term clients. Municipal officials are firmly opposed to the addition of new public housing facilities and, indeed, of subsidized facilities of any kind. While lip-service is given to the cause of housing people with limited income, the functional reality, as seen in most of the building that had been proposed within the city, is for high-cost luxury housing.

The bewilderment of state officials who must deal with the political realities of the city is mirrored in the remarks made by Philip Caton in the course of a long interview. Caton, the assistant commissioner of the New Jersey Department of Community Affairs, had been delegated to oversee state participation in the efforts to develop modestly priced shelter within Atlantic City. Proposals for infill housing on vacant lots, for manufactured homes, for assuming site acquisition costs, and for arranging Section 235 financing (a low-interest mortgage homeownership program) followed one after the other. Sites were identified, plans were drawn up, and then suddenly, Commissioner Caton explained, "the Mayor decided that there was a better use for all of the sites. Nothing to date has happened on any of these sites. There is a point at which the state has to back off." Caton summarized his feelings: "There is now incredible frustration on the housing issue. Further commitment by the state will depend upon some meetings of the minds, a mutual understanding of its role in redevelopment."[25]

Perhaps the observation by Matthew McCool, director of the city's community development, explains the difficulty. The city "exceeded its fair share formula housing allocations [the New

Jersey plan allocating low-income units throughout the state] by 35 percent in 1978, and that was for the target year 1990. We have talked to the people at HUD and they feel that Atlantic City has more than its share of low-income housing."[26] Atlantic City was a community of poor people before the casinos and, at least to some in the city, of too many poor people. The advent of new economic vitality is seen by one sector as an opportunity to reduce this "excess."

Nor is there much relief in shelter costs anywhere within Atlantic County. Housing prices have escalated at a ferocious rate in almost all of the surrounding communities. (See Table 21.) The precasino stagnation of Atlantic City's housing market is reflected in the low median sales price of 1972 – $13,500. By 1976, the median sales price increased by only 11.1 percent, the smallest rate of increase in any of the municipalities listed, raising it to only the $15,000 level. From 1976 to 1980, however, the median sales price more than doubled to $37,000. Compared with the median sales prices of existing single-family homes sold in the entire Northeast, which stood at $60,800 in 1980, it is still a relatively modest figure. But, unfortunately, the modesty is more a reflection of the scabrous condition of the housing, since much of it trades for underlying land values rather than for shelter.

From the viewpoint of those who see housing as investment or speculation and were fortunate enough to have prior holdings, Table 21 is a thing of beauty. To those who were the beneficiaries of relatively inexpensive rentals based upon low values and poor markets, the figures are a disaster. Two young casino dealers, each earning $25,000 a year and sharing housing accommodations, can afford the nearly $100,000 price tag that is attached to reasonable private housing in the city and its suburban areas; the welfare recipient or those dependent on social security cannot. But to whom should the city be dedicated? The population of Atlantic City that was? Or is? Or might be?

The head of the Atlantic City NAACP, Pierre Hollingsworth, viewed the product of all of these misadventures and misdeeds as creating "an Atlantic City for the filthy rich and the filthy poor." He echoed the fears of the black and Spanish-speaking population when he added, "They don't want us here. They are constantly [saying] the land is too valuable for people to live here. They mean us."[27]

Planning for Growth

The exasperating task of anticipating how large the new population will be – a task that must be performed in order to build for it – is tied to the issues related to the changing makeup of the population. A sensible next step after arriving at a realistic population projection is to create a master plan.

Planning for every element of Atlantic City's future has been skewed by conflicting forecasts: casinos will multiply endlessly, or the casino business will die before it has time to take root. In no area are the projections more diverse than efforts to provide forecasts of demand for households and dwelling units.

The Casino Control Commission has held endless hearings on the subject. Mayor Joseph Lazarow of Atlantic City conveyed a sense of the limitations and frustrations of municipal authorities at hearings held on February 28, 1980. There was no parameter of growth, whether housing, sewers, water supply, or transportation, for which he did not indicate overwhelming need. At the same time, his testimony demonstrated an obvious lack of clearly defined targets or hard commitments. In terms of the housing supply, for example, he suggested a need for 8,000 to 10,000 housing units within the city over the next ten years. When pushed by one of the commissioners, he indicated that it might very well be 20,000 additional housing units.[28]

Economic Research Associates, the consulting firm employed by the Atlantic City Housing Authority and Urban Redevelopment Agency, estimated that, given eight casinos by 1985, there would be between 23,300 and 30,800 total households within the city. Two years later, the same consulting firm, assuming twenty casinos by 1985, produced a forecast of only 21,950 households; that is, more casinos yet fewer households generated by their employees and those of associated businesses. The state Department of Community Affairs produced household projections approximately a third higher than those of Economic Research Associates for the same year This forecast was based upon only eight casinos, yet it represented *twice* as many households as there were in 1980, when there were already six casinos.

The overlay of governmental institutions that play (or attempt to play) a role in Atlantic City has produced incredible confusion. Many of these agencies have issued their own demographic projections, all of which differ enormously. With so many different governmental agencies making decisions that affect growth and development in the area, there is still no central forum, formal or informal, in which to discuss and coordinate policy activities.

Once again, this reflects the political realities and rival aspirations of the varied groups within the city. The state, at least in theory, should stand above the fray, but it has refused to take central responsibility. In the face of a massive alteration in the city's job base and economic function, that decision has proved costly to Atlantic City's resident poor.

While New Jersey's Municipal Land Use Law does not require a municipality to have a master plan – a general document establishing long-range, broad parameters that guide future growth – it does establish the basis upon which the specifics of zoning ordinances can be developed. The courts will not uphold local zoning ordinances if they are not based upon a municipally adopted land-use plan, an integral part of a full master plan. Atlantic City has spent the better part of $1 million developing its master plan, although it virtually excludes housing as a primary topic. Discussions with a number of people involved with developing the plan as well as knowledgeable observers suggest that it represents a careful avoidance of an issue that is too controversial to be brought to the surface.

But avoiding specifics in the provision of housing by municipalities is certainly not unique to Atlantic City. Most suburban communities in the state, and possibly even in the nation as a whole, seem to follow this practice. Instead of instituting any methodical approach to complementing job growth with the development of shelter accommodations, Atlantic City has cried out, "Let's get the casinos to do it!" This has become the verbal escape hatch of practically all the governmental authorities involved with housing in Atlantic City.

The various pulls and tugs within the state have combined to frustrate development efforts. A massive restriction of land use within the Pinelands limits the development of nearly 90 percent of the county. The state sewer-expansion plan seems to have been made without reference to its own projections of future demand within the county.[29]

Charles Worthington, the Atlantic County executive, pointed out the failure of the state to provide a common meeting ground or, for that matter, even to clarify the specific role that casinos or the taxes derived from them are to play in the housing arena. He also raised the issue of whether the state's role should be something more than that of critic: "If the state persists in spending most of its time in acting as a regulatory agency and too little time in acting as the source of assistance in providing infrastructure, then the casino dream will become everyone's nightmare."[30]

Atlantic City does not merely share the common national problems associated with delivering housing – the situation is accentuated there. The state allowed the casinos to open in an area where much of the land potentially available within the city had been diverted by speculation into nonuse, while peripheral areas were zoned out of the market by state intervention. The results have been an escalation in the cost of buildable land.

The state government has abdicated its responsibilities and its prereferendum promises. As Peter Tucci, president of the New Jersey Builders' Association, said, "The housing crisis in Atlantic City existed long before the introduction of casino gambling in the area. But very little was being done to force housing production prior to the advent of casino gambling; next to nothing has been done since."[31] Tucci pointed to rent-control regulations in Atlantic County as inhibiting development of dwelling units; the state legislature has refused to enact a uniform rent-control act, thus leaving development to the vagaries of local government.

Casino officials are bewildered observers and participants in this process. In the words of one of them, "I have been here for two years and I've seen in government: disunity, fragmentation and a deep-seated animosity. There is no cooperation and coordination. Mandrake the Magician couldn't get anything done here. They would drive Mandrake crazy."[32]

In the face of negative publicity regarding the failure to provide a support structure for the city, the governor appointed a special cabinet-level task force, but it has done nothing. It was supposed to be the highest state body dealing with issues related to Atlantic City's problems but, in the words of one of the participants in the commission, "the cabinet committee meetings quickly became staff workshops as cabinet level people do not attend; staffers of the various state agencies attempted to coordinate activities in Atlantic City."[33] There was no real push from the governor's office, so perhaps the task force was never intended to be more than window dressing. A burst of government press releases could not conceal the nonproductive nature of the exercise.

The Casinos' Responsibility

The goal initially espoused for gaming and a key to its passage was the rehabilitation of Atlantic City. The basic concept in the original casino enabling legislation, as further elaborated in the administrative codes that have followed, is the explicit requirement that the casinos accept a measure of responsibility for the whole environment, which clearly includes housing. The question of whether the casinos have a responsibility for the direct provision of housing or for generating funds to be given to public bodies that, in turn, will divert some of them to housing support has yet to be resolved. The record is very unclear on this point.

The casinos have shown contradictory attitudes. They show an eagerness to be "good citizens," but they also disclaim responsibility. In the words of the executive director of the Atlantic City Casino Hotel Association, William Downey, "Government is asking industry to do their [government's] job. The state invited the industry here to run gaming houses, not to do transportation, housing, sewers."[34]

A senior executive of one of the gaming casinos expressed a common point of view: "We want to be helpful but we don't want to go out and build housing. We are looked to because we are the most visible entity – we are a casino/hotel and resort company. That is our experience, persuasion, and objective. We are not housing developers. We recognize that the city's housing problem creates a problem for us; it is a problem for our workforce – remember that the city had a housing problem before casinos."[35]

The actual power of the Casino Control Commission to impose housing-development requirements on the casinos is not clearly defined in the Casino Control Act, which merely suggests that the commission analyze the impact of the casinos in terms of the local ecology, with housing cited as a "grave area."[36] The real power of the commission, however, lies in the fact that even a permanent license requires annual renewal. Thus "the casino license is for one year. Naturally we listen to the Casino Control Commission."[37] But to listen is not necessarily to act.

The commission unquestionably influences the casinos, but it does so on a hit-or-miss basis, without an underlying policy. The ad hoc nature of the commission's involvement in housing is indicated in a statement by one administrator about securing funding for housing from Resorts International: "When we saw how much money Resorts was making, it seemed inordinate. We decided that we would hit them up for a major commitment to housing. We asked for $7 million figuring that we would get $5 million and that's just what we got."[38] The bulk of this investment has been spent by Resorts in Atlantic County joint ventures. There is some reserve for action in Atlantic City, but it is all on land that is encumbered by a variety of title problems. In order to build on these lands, an enormous number of government agencies must provide clearance. The inability to obtain the needed clearances, indeed the lack of clarity as to who should do so, leaves these ventures in limbo.

Joseph Lordi, when he was the Casino Control Commission chairman, pointed out that the commission is limited to encouraging Atlantic City's hotel firms to contribute to housing development within the city limits as well as bringing the problem to the public's attention. He did state, however, that the commission could choose to delay or defer casino license applications until sufficient housing is available for employees.[39] It should be noted that when the Resorts International license renewal came up in the spring of 1981, the operator agreed to commit an additional $1 million to a low- and moderate-income housing project in the city.[40] Why $1 million rather than $2 million – or none? Such financial commitments may be acts of noblesse oblige or the payments of administrative blackmail. And the money secured from Resorts for housing to date is an isolated event, not the result of policy.

Casinos not only failed to solve the housing problem that existed before the referendum, but the city's housing stock has degenerated in the period since the casinos were initiated. Lordi himself stressed that "things were bad then; they're worse now."[41] The pressures of a boomtown are enormous. In the words of Hollingsworth of Atlantic City's NAACP, "Every time they [the casinos] open up, they bring people to town – we cannot handle the situation the way it's going now."[42] Samuel Seldon, the deputy director of welfare rights of Atlantic City, stated the problem this way: "What are you going to do about the people who are coming in every day? They're getting good jobs in the casinos. Housing that we have here, the low income family can't afford. They [the newcomers] are taking up all the housing."[43]

When Resorts' gross win in its first year without competition was an unparalleled quarter of a billion dollars, the major concern of the state was whether it had secured a large enough share of the take. As noted elsewhere in this book, efforts were made to raise the state tax on the win as well as to increase emphasis on the possibilities of "shaking down" the casinos for more public-facility funding. But as one Casino Control Commission official noted, "By the time we got around to talking with them [the casinos], business was bad. It just didn't seem like the right time, particularly in the light of the number of potential casino openings faltering, to push for a special commitment."[44]

As competition stiffened and gross win figures in 1980 began to disappoint analysts, the counterpressures from the casinos began to rise, not merely for a reduction in regulation but also in terms of their explicit and implicit requirements to contribute funding for housing and other forms of development. The director of the Atlantic City Casino Hotel Commission, for example, in testifying before the Casino Control Commission in January 1980, pointed to up-front costs of more than $100 million per casino opening: "For us to assess any one of our developers who are in that planning stage with up-front costs, additional up-front costs, I think we jeopardize the financial feasibility of our investment and would be counterproductive. This is especially so, Commissioner, when you consider there are a number of other jurisdictions that are looking at this question of gaming now."[45] The casino operators are masters of the carrot and the stick.

At the time, Assistant Commissioner Kenneth N. MacDonald (later to be indicted in the Abscam investigations), while raising the question, "how can development of community services keep pace with the expected rate of industry development?" emphasized the importance of "particular sensitivity to the need of a casino industry during critical capital formation stage. The housing and other infrastructure requirements of the community . . . must be balanced by the economic reality that if Atlantic City is to reap the benefits of redevelopment, sufficient capital commitment and construction must be made prior to the establishment of the casino gaming in competing jurisdictions."[46]

The casinos are required by law to pay a 2 percent reinvestment tax to "benefit the public good" through investment in land development and housing in the area, or to pay an equivalent tax to the state. Despite the fact that the very scale of the 2 percent tax, as well as the elements that would qualify in lieu of direct payment, is unclear (see Chapter 6), the debate on its utilization has been substantial. For example, Philip Caton, then the director of the Division of Housing and Community Affairs, who had served on the governor's task force, believes it should be invested in projects that address the fundamental needs of the community. He includes in this not only housing but also transportation, health-care facilities, and educational facilities.[47]

But a variety of forces are driving this potential expenditure into convention facilities rather than housing. The Atlantic City convention business has experienced substantial attrition. Critics have commented that the limited number of first-class hotel rooms prohibits securing prestige conventions, and there is no question that the present convention hall is a relic of days long past – it is simply not competitive. Assemblyman Michael

Matthews, Democrat from Atlantic County and viewed as a spokesman for the casinos, has currently proposed the expansion and rehabilitation of the hall. The source of funds to cover the costs to support the new convention center will divert money that had been earlier earmarked for housing.[48]

In any case, at this writing, only Resorts International (which is already heavily involved in land and housing projects) and Caesars Boardwalk Regency are facing the tax reinvestment issue, though others will soon join them.

Housing in the Casino Era

The community dreamed of a revival. The poor envisioned not only jobs but improvements in housing conditions and transportation facilities. The reality is that the costs of support structures, the fear of competition, and the need to complement the casinos with additional sources of pulling power have combined to leave many of the "softer" amenities lagging in the background. These amenities have much in the way of emotional support, but little political support.

There has been a gross understatement of the needs of the city and for public investment of profits from the casinos. There has been a corresponding overstatement of the largesse anticipated from casino gaming and the speed with which it would be delivered. "Legalized casino gaming is the fastest and probably the cheapest form of urban renewal yet created by the capitalist system," according to a market analyst at Paine-Webber.[49] But the rewards to the precasino population have been slight – and not because of a lack of appropriate legislation. All casino applicants are required by statute to submit to the Casino Control Commission impact statements that include not only their proposed architecture and site plans, in accord with the master plan, local zoning, and planning ordinances of Atlantic City, but also an analysis of the effect of their proposal on the overall environment, including economic, social, demographic, and competitive conditions in Atlantic City and the state of New Jersey.[50]

Proposals for housing projects result from this procedure, but they rarely get past this stage. The Atlantic City Department of

Planning has reviewed all the projects that had been proposed since the advent of the casinos. As of July 1982, only 864 subsidized housing units had been completed since 1978. An additional 468 units of subsidized housing for the elderly and 292 nonsubsidized condominium units were under construction. Of all the completed projects since 1978, fewer than half were for nonelderly families.[51] And most of these projects had been started, or at least planned, before casino development was under way. New developments that have been proposed are for luxury housing. In the meantime, while the market dreams of new facilities at the very top tier of rents and prices, the number of extant housing units at more modest levels continues to diminish. In the words of one government administrator, "The town government doesn't want low-income housing. They are just going through the motions despite the efforts of the Casino Control Commission and the Atlantic Housing Corporation."[52]

A new form of government has been adopted within the city that, for the first time, permits a popularly elected mayor. It remains to be seen, however, whether this will alter the basic pressures that have been exerted against the continued occupancy in Atlantic City by low- and moderate-income households. Is the golden gleam of the casinos and a desire to attract the richer visitor antithetical to the continuance of Atlantic City as a refuge for the less fortunate in our society? The state has carefully avoided coming to grips with this problem. The failure to undertake advance planning and establish priorities before the coming of the casinos continues to exact a substantial toll.

The casinos have seemingly generated substantial public revenues. Yet these are radically overstated. What is left in their wake is a cluster of unmet community needs that, far from dwindling in the casinos' presence, have been accentuated. The state has skimmed the cream off the income and left behind a mass of unpaid bills.

Casino gaming's promise of rejuvenation is most attractive to areas that have long felt the stings of blight – not least in housing. This is a common denominator among the several locations that have been in the forefront of the progambling movement. Although much was promised on the housing front prior to the casinos, the Atlantic City experience indicates that their advent may be far from an unmixed blessing. Is the housing shortfall of Atlantic City caused by conditions unique to that community, or are there lessons here for other jurisdictions considering casino gaming? The potential level of displacement that would be engendered in Long Beach, Long Island, which now serves as a sanctuary for many mainstreamed former patients of mental institutions in New York State, would be appalling. The ecology of such a location may be the despair of the local chamber of commerce, but the full implications of dynamiting it by the creation of casinos must be kept in mind.

Similarly, the southern area of Miami Beach, long deserted by the fashionable and left as a retirement community for elderly northeasterners, particularly from New York City's garment industry, is viewed by local realty interests as a blighted area ripe for casino-induced redevelopment. While the virtues of dynamic growth are many, they must be viewed within a wider context, including the need to rehouse those with the least mobility, based on both age and income. Without this perspective, the nominal economic and fiscal vigor created by casinos is vastly overstated – the real victims are those displaced by the boom. This perspective has been lacking in Atlantic City.

The advent of the casinos occurred when the housing industry of the United States as a whole was severely hit by unparalleled increases in mortgage costs. In turn, this made the provision of housing difficult even for middle-income individuals. Within that stricture, however, a number of general observations can be made. First and foremost among them is the failure of government to comprehend the level of real-estate speculation and, with it, forced displacement that the casinos would cause. Glorious views of the future served as inadequate surrogates for carefully developed plans.

The state administration was in a position of granting a unique and valuable monopoly, which could have served as a bargaining tool to establish a regional plan incorporating not only Atlantic City but its environs. This was not done. The passage of the casino-enabling legislation, the pressures to develop rapidly, and then to ensure that additional casinos would be added as quickly as possible further weakened the state's bargaining capacities. Though efforts are being made to redress the balance, they are probably too late. The very success of Atlantic City's casinos makes its land too expensive, its prospects too alluring, to accommodate the low-incomed. To reverse this reality would have taken a level of government commitment that is nonexistent.

Overlaying these facts is the issue of the future shape of the cityand its environs. The order of priorities that would have brought a genuine revival of the city as a diverse residential area has been largely ignored. The reasons why these mistakes were made – and the possibility that such mistakes are inevitable – are important for other areas considering legalization.

CRIME

Americans are fascinated by crime, unless it is in their own backyard. The vision of Nevada as haven for mob activities is one of the dominant folk themes of our time, and this traditional linkage of crime and criminals to gaming did hurt initial efforts to win acceptance of casino gaming in New Jersey. The fear of crime still causes the greatest apprehension when the advisability of legalized casino gambling is considered. In a survey by *Gambling Business Magazine*, the principal reason the eleven governors who responded gave for the general lack of enthusiasm for expanding gaming to their states was crime and the inevitable influx of "unsavory elements."[1]

The fear was sharpened in New Jersey by the unhappy image of the state as one that had already long harbored criminal elements. In a study of the economics of gambling, conducted by the Bureau of Business and Economic Research of the University of Nevada, the author pointed to New Jersey, in terms of its location, as the epitome of a state that could successfully legalize casinos. On the other hand, he suggested that "New Jersey has been plagued by scandals in government in recent years and thus would probably have difficulty . . . in preventing organized crime from infiltrating legalized gaming operations."[2]

When legalization was approved, a vast apparatus of rhetoric and enforcement was put in place in Atlantic City to control casino-related crime. How well has it worked? Is there a skimming off of casino wins in order to avoid taxes and to finance a variety of illicit operations? Given the nature of criminal activity, the record is not available for casual examination. But enough information can be derived from the limited data available to give some indication of the magnitude of the problem. The final tally is far from clear, and what evidence we have must be viewed with considerable caution. It must be placed within the context not only of business behavior as a whole (taking care of the cop on the beat so that you can park your truck illegally to deliver goods is an old established custom) but also of the sudden shower of wealth that has poured over Atlantic City.

From the viewpoint of the city's chief of police, it is this new wealth that accounts for some of the unfair disrepute of casino gaming in the city. "People like to talk about casino-related crime. I don't really like the phrase, for the simple reason that . . . [the increase in crime] . . . could be related to any kind of economic growth. If somebody discovered oil, discovered gold, the same thing would happen."[3] To the head of the Division of Gaming Enforcement, G. Michael Brown, however, the casinos do attract criminals and crime: "Casinos seek to be treated like any other business . . . [but] they aren't any other business. They never have been and they never will be. They are unique in the purpose they serve and the threat they pose."[4] Reconciling the realities to these differing interpretations will clarify the extent and nature of crime in Atlantic City.

Statistics on crime vary enormously from place to place. Studies indicate, for example, that the incidence of reporting by crime victims may differ by as much as 300 percent between communities, without even taking into account the vagaries of tabulation. Leaving that problem aside, studies show that although Las Vegas experiences a higher-than-average incidence of murder, rape, robbery, and burglary compared to the nation as a whole, its crime rates are roughly comparable to those of similar cities and other resort areas.[5]

The development of the Atlantic City casinos caused a host of undesirables to flock into the community and its immediate environs. A stroll along the boardwalk confirms the prevalence of prostitutes and others eager to relieve the winners of their gains – or to provide some form of solace to the losers. Since the start of casinos in 1978, and despite a strengthened police force, the growth in the crime index of Atlantic City has far exceeded that of the state as a whole. (See Table 22.) The 1979 to 1980 increase of 69.7 percent is seven times that experienced by New Jersey.

Atlantic City's overall crime rate per 1000 persons declined from 1970 through the immediate precasino years. But this was quickly reversed. By 1980, there was a crime committed for every four persons resident in the city, five times the number for the state. An examination of specific crimes for Atlantic City alone indicates prodigious increases. (See Table 23.) From 1977 to 1981, there was a near tripling of total crimes, with larcenies in every form joining with robbery and assault at the crest of the wave.[6] Even Newark's crime rate, heavy as it is, pales by comparison.

The provision of illegal goods and services, including drugs, prostitution, loansharking, bookmaking, and sports betting, is a traditional criminal activity. The commerce in drugs not only involves organized crime but also individuals and groups only tenuously connected or related to the criminal establishment. The drug traffic has picked up in the city. There is reportedly open buying and selling of drugs just blocks away from the casinos. As one community resident stated, "I've lived in Atlantic City for thirty-three years, and I can't remember when it's been so open – that when you walk down Kentucky Avenue you are solicited for drugs and stolen merchandise."[7]

There have been shootouts by rival gangs involved in the drug trade; and in the spring of 1981, eleven people were indicted for their alleged involvement in a narcotics ring operating from the Coral Reef Lounge of the Montego Bay Motel. The supposed head and two other members of the ring were former members of the roofers union, Local 30. Also named, but not indicted, were two Atlantic City police officers who were accused of receiving payments to protect the ring.[8]

Controversy surrounds the association of top officials in the Atlantic City Police Department with known criminals. Police were withdrawn from surveillance just before a shootout in a roller disco between two rival gangs involved in the drug trade. Suspicions have been voiced that the information was leaked from the police department. One experienced county investigator summarized a not wholly unique point of view when he said, "there have always been problems in that department [the police] but I have never seen it this bad before . . . The association with criminals by key personnel, coupled with the narcotics arrests, is a major problem."[9]

The crime data are only partly a result of the vast increase in the transient population, including criminals, attracted to Atlantic City from relatively close urban areas. They are also the result of the drastic social dislocations caused by sudden wealth in the midst of continued poverty. The spillover of casino largess has been limited, displacement has broken the tenuous lines of neighborhoods, and many find criminal activity an irresistible way to share in the new wealth they see all around them. But it is the issue of organized crime, not street crime and prostitution, that most troubles observers in the state and elsewhere.

Organized crime clearly dominated casino gaming in Nevada for many years, and this supports the belief that the tables and slot machines in Atlantic City must have brought with them criminal figures from the past. Such individuals have a capacity for suborning government, for using the cash and favors of the casinos to go outside the law, and for avoiding whatever paper restrictions are nominally put on casino operations. Many believe that the casinos are used to secure illegal flows of funds by which criminal activities can be financed and to "launder" illegally obtained funds.

The vendor issue illustrates the problem of organized crime and the casinos. Criminal involvement, or the involvement of criminals (they are not the same thing), in the vending-machine business as well as in the wholesale and retail distribution of liquor has strong antecedents in New Jersey and elsewhere. The taint of criminal connections among vendors for linens, trucking, laundry, food, cigarettes, and liquor is not new. Similarly, the organizers and controllers of the unions whose members staff the casinos have had a checkered history.

Therefore, in approaching the question of crime in the casinos or among the service vendors, the baseline of traditional American business practices must be addressed. One high government official, who was central to the development of the casino regulations, pointed to the fact that criminal elements are entrenched in the service industries. He raised the issue of whether "it makes a hell of a lot of difference if your laundry is syndicate-controlled or if a casino's laundry is syndicate-controlled?"[10] In his estimation, the casinos have not significantly altered the basic relationships. Casino gambling in Atlantic City may present nothing more than an enlargement of the market, a sudden boomtown bonanza for vendors, both corrupt and otherwise.

The vending issue is complex. The demand for cigarette machines in high-traffic sites is substantial. A pattern exists within the restaurant industry of cigarette distributors who serve as sources of substantial front money to restaurants and nightclubs in order to secure choice locations. For example, front-money payment in excess of $25,000 was made available on very generous terms in return for the exclusive rights to cigarette machines within a relatively small Manhattan bar and grill.[11]

The same pattern holds true for many vendors of restaurant supplies. One of the major vendors in New York City was famous as a source of funds for seasoned restaurant entrepreneurs who wanted to open new facilities. In return for a loan, the restaurateur would agree to buy all of his coffee and certain other products through the moneylender's distributorship.

Whether the product is linen services or fresh fruits and vegetables, the capacity to borrow against future purchases has been key to the front-end financing and fixturing of the restaurant and nightclub business. Even leases of hatcheck installations or franchises for manning the doors at popular places have served as bankable elements to be capitalized through the services of moneylenders, sometimes for lump payments or more commonly for loans. The loans are typically written at nominal interest rates but sometimes include "juice," payoffs in cash or services that are not visible to the tax collector. The step from this type of arrangement to simple extortion can be relatively short.

The State of New Jersey Commission of Investigation looked at the incursions by organized crime into certain legitimate businesses in Atlantic City. While there is a stringent licensing requirement for services that directly cater to the casino hotel complex, there are additional important issues, at least in the commission's estimation, relating to organized crime in the city which cannot be addressed appropriately within the Casino Control Act itself. One of these is cigarette vending.

In the course of public hearings, the Commission discovered that Angelo Bruno, "the reputed head of organized crime in Philadelphia" (Bruno was killed shortly afterward), served as a salesman in a firm called John's Wholesale Distributors of Philadelphia. The firm applied for a retail cigarette distributorship in Atlantic City within a few days after the passage of the gambling referendum. The hearings established that Bruno received a commission for every pack of cigarettes sold by the wholesale outlet, regardless of whether he had secured that business for the company. In addition, he obtained significant retail machine locations within the city on his own account. Bruno contended that his vending interests in Atlantic City were limited, but documentary evidence confirmed that John's Wholesale Distributors had tripled its business since taking him on as a "salesman." The investigation highlighted the fact that neither the licensing of cigarette vendors nor securing a license for the distribution of alcoholic beverages involved investigations of possible criminal connections or, for that matter, previous jail sentences of applicants or owners. Further testimony showed that Bruno owned a major bar and restaurant in Atlantic City, the Casanova Disco, in conjunction with the Gambino brothers, who were cousins and associates of the late Carlo Gambino, often referred to as one of the principal criminal bosses in the United States.

The casualness with which the state's Alcoholic Beverages Commission administers its duty was reflected by the testimony of

Commissioner Bryant of that organization, who stated that the commission simply processed papers and had not done any investigation into prior criminal records and possible disqualifications of owners. He further acknowledged that the application form had a number of sections left blank, the form was not notarized, and a corporate seal was not affixed. He candidly admitted it was impossible for the Alcohol Beverages Control Unit in Atlantic City to discharge its responsibilities under the state's Enabling Act because of inadequate staffing.[12]

Reading through the recommendations of the New Jersey Commission of Investigation and its call for a thorough reform of licensing procedures, one cannot escape the feeling that what has been impugned and indicted is not gaming, but rather a pattern of business that gives potential access to organized crime. The casinos, therefore, are to some degree mainly repeating American business behavior that has a very long history. This interpretation is further illustrated by the issues of shakedowns during the course of casino construction and labor racketeering.

Extortion and Labor

On large-scale construction sites in New York City, 5 percent of total costs are not uncommonly set aside to pay for an "expeditor." While much of the expeditor's activity may involve purely legal efforts to speedily secure permits, licenses, and the like, there is general consensus that sometimes an equal amount of time and money goes directly or indirectly to ensuring labor peace on the construction site.

Given the enormous costs of a casino facility, the price of delay is staggering, and making hidden payments to outsiders or insiders becomes enticing. Although any corporation can be driven to overpaying a consultant or lawyer who acts as its distributor, the casinos, deluged with cash, which enhances the opportunities for payoffs in nontraceable money, may be even more tempted to follow this road, buying labor peace, avoiding taxes, and in the end financing criminal activities.

In Atlantic City, a number of casino developers experienced brief labor stoppages or slowdowns as their buildings neared completion. Whether these were matters resolved by legitimate bargaining or by some measure of payoff is unclear. The state's attorney general, James Zazzali, in the course of asking the Assembly to give state gaming regulators powers to review and approve casino construction contracts, pointed out that "we all know that in the construction phase of any project, the pressures of construction completion creates the opportunity for commercial extortion and the intrusion of criminal elements."[13] During the same hearing, Director Brown of the Division of Gaming Enforcement indicated that two incidents of possible impropriety in dealings with casinos during the construction phase were under investigation.

There is substantial evidence that people with known criminal backgrounds have a significant stake in some of the major construction firms in and around Atlantic City. One of them, Nicky Scarfo, was most recently found innocent of murder charges in the gangland-style slaying of a major cement contractor in the area. Scarfo is viewed as the new head of the Angelo Bruno crime family.[14] It is interesting to note that Scarfo's nephew, Philip Leonetti, operates a concrete company that in turn has been a subcontractor on three casino projects.[15]

In testimony before a special casino-control hearing, G. Robert Blakey, head of the University of Notre Dame's Organized Crime Institute, gave a possible scenario for the use of labor unions as leverage against the casinos by organized crime: "Labor peace . . . the guarantee of no-strikes or disruption of service . . . can be arranged through a direct under the table payment to corrupt union heads and mobsters or through agreements extracted under pressure that the casinos contract for services with a certain maintenance firm, laundry service, law firm, architect, consultant . . . that are now under control by the mob."[16]

The Philadelphia roofers' union, Local 30, which was headed by John McCullough before he was murdered, is actively involved in labor organizing in Atlantic City. Local 30, a union with a reputation for militant, sometimes violent behavior, took over Local 230, a small roofers' union in Atlantic City, when legalization was approved. McCullough was also closely associated with leaders of the International Brotherhood of Security Officers, Local 40B, which was attempting to organize casino security guards. When McCullough was murdered, it was theorized that it may have been because of his connection to the Bruno crime organization. Bruno's Philadelphia group was opposed by a New York organization with a questionable background, which was also trying to organize the security guards.[17]

Another union, Local 54 of the Hotel, Restaurant and Country Club Employees Union, which represents hotel, casino, and restaurant workers in the Atlantic City area, has been the object of investigation by the New Jersey Department of Gaming Enforcement.[18] In May 1981, the attorney general asked the Casino Control Commission to deny registration to Local 54, claiming that it had been infiltrated by organized crime. Its secretary-treasurer, Robert Lumio, was convicted in 1974 on federal gambling charges and is also thought to be an associate of Nicky Scarfo's. At the same time, the state attorney general is concerned about the background of some of Atlantic City's security-guard unions.[19] The Casino Control Commission's capacity to oust the union (and the state's authority over the unions) has been challenged by Local 54. As of this writing, the union has not been replaced, and the issue of the state's jurisdiction over unions will have a long fight in a variety of courts.

Meanwhile, an epidemic of murder has broken out in Philadelphia's crime circles, long the overlords of Atlantic City. Beginning in March 1980 with the murder of Angelo Bruno, there have been a number of other murders in an evident fight for succession. Philip C. Testa, who took over the leadership of the Philadelphia organization after Bruno's death, was killed in March 1981, and at least four or five other mob members were shot to death in the interim. McCullough of Local 30 was shot in December 1980. The Pennsylvania Crime Commission, in its decennial report issued in 1980, noted: "The number of deaths of organized crime figures and associates which occurred during the past year is unprecedented in the state."[20]

The general consensus of informed observers is that these murders point both to internecine conflict within the Philadelphia organization and to a fight between the latter and New York and Chicago crime organizations over which group will control criminal activity in Atlantic City. The most widely accepted theory, now reported as circulating among law-enforcement groups, is that the Genovese and Gambino New York crime groups are seeking to control the Philadelphia organization and, through it, Atlantic City. Just how valid these observations are is far from certain. But as a Philadelphia labor leader stated in response to the death of John McCullough: "You don't have to go outside . . . to know . . . it's snowing."[21]

In the land of hearsay and "authoritative" newspaper stories, it is difficult to maintain a perspective. The *Chicago Tribune*, for example, ran a feature article on a six-hour conclave attended by top families of the nation's crime syndicates in Philadelphia, which supposedly divided up the profits from illegal ventures, as well as legitimate businesses, growing out of gambling in Atlantic City. According to the article, Chicago members were given free reign in Las Vegas and, in turn, the New York families secured hegemony over Atlantic City.[22]

But what does seem to be beyond dispute is that Scarfo has succeeded two generations of murdered predecessors as head of the Philadelphia family. According to charges filed by the FBI, about three years ago Angelo Bruno had delegated Scarfo to "seek control for the Bruno family of ancillary services for Atlantic City's hotels, including the supplying of meat, glassware and laundry services." At the same time, another Bruno associate was put in charge of gaining control of Local 54. When Scarfo's home was raided by police in December 1979, telephone numbers and other material showed a close association not only with other members of the Bruno family, but also with the Gambino, Genovese, and Columbo families of New York City.[23]

Should we blame the casinos for luring mobsters to Atlantic City? Certainly there is nothing on the record indicating that they have done anything more than any other large-scale developer, that is, hiring those who can assure performance while perhaps not looking too closely at backgrounds.

But casino gaming in its practices as well as its antecedents has special problems that are not merely the common inheritance of large-scale business enterprises. The relationship between casinos and illegal activities can be traced to the involvement of gaming entrepreneurs with the Teamsters and the Teamsters' Pension Fund. Lurking within this alliance is the omnipresent but elusive Meyer Lansky, international gaming entrepreneur, who seems to have had the key to the Teamster vault. Lansky, whose association with organized crime dates back to Prohibition days, had long been involved with major gambling efforts both in the United States and abroad.[24]

It is important to remember that casino gaming's history of banking respectability is relatively brief. Until the last six or seven years, traditional sources of institutional capital kept their distance. In Nevada, a regulation existed requiring that each stockholder of a casino be individually licensed. Since securing individual licensing for every stockholder of a publicly traded company was virtually impossible, this prevented public corporations from owning gaming facilities and until 1969 eliminated conventional equity investors as a source of funds.[25]

It was the Teamsters' Central States Pension Fund that was the major source of capital for the casinos; it was responsible for much of Las Vegas' development. As late as 1978, $247 million out of $1.5 billion in Teamster pension assets were invested in Nevada casinos. It was only in the 1970s, when gaming was coming of age as a big business, that bankers became willing to make loans to casinos. "Going public" became necessary in order to cash in the equity that had been built up in the casino hotels.

Sweetheart deals were made using the pension funds of the Teamsters at rates well below market and, therefore, involving a fraud perpetrated against pension contributors. The ties between Caesars World, owned by the Perlman brothers, later to be ousted from Atlantic City, and Alvin Malnik, Lansky's lieutenant, existed as late as 1976. A *Rouge et Noir* report details a pattern of sales and leasebacks arranged by Malnik, lubricated by Teamster funds, which yielded very generous capital gains for the go-between's services.[26]

The connection of Caesars World, Malnik, and Lansky is described with precision in a March 5, 1976, report by the audit division of the Nevada Gaming Commission and Control Board. One transaction involved resorts in Pennsylvania which, with midwifing of the Teamsters' Pension Fund, yielded Malnik a profit in excess of $10 million and Caesars a low cash-drain investment. This occurred after two prior Nevada commission warnings to Caesars to discontinue its involvement with Malnik.[27] Caesars was found unqualified for a New Jersey casino license by the Casino Control Commission because of the alleged criminal associations of the Perlman brothers, its founders and principal stockholders. The Perlmans were forced to sell their interest in the parent company in both Nevada and New Jersey.

The finding of the Superior Court of New Jersey's Appellate Division seems very clear-cut in upholding the powers of the Casino Control Commission. The Perlmans' presence was found reason enough for the denial because of "their apparent continuing insensitivity to a potential impact of those associations in this sensitive industry" (referring to the findings of the Nevada Gaming Commission.[28]) The court affirms the necessity for a casino license applicant to have a higher level of morality than holds true for business as a whole: "The question which the Perlmans failed to see then and, perhaps understandably, do not now acknowledge, is: what of the impact of those transactions and associations upon the policies intended to be served by casino gaming regulation under legislative imprimatur? . . . Good character in the sense here appropriate is deemed to refer to conduct not potentially detrimental to the industry."[29] The cost to the Perlmans and to their company may be measured in the tens of millions.

The problem is not confined to Caesars World. The Del Webb Corporation, for example, as well as several of its key executives, is under indictment for conspiracy to defraud the Teamsters' Central States Pension Fund of a million dollars on a construction project involving one of the major Las Vegas hotels. The company has been forced to sell its share of its Atlantic City casino.

The Credit Question

The liberal credit practices of the casino business, at least in Nevada and New Jersey, are one reason why the industry is so appealing to organized crime. Of course, there are legitimate reasons for offering credit. "You need credit for the same reason a guy . . . [does who] buys a million dollar yacht, or a $5,000 car.

Gambling is recreation or sport, the same as sailing . . . It is a credit society and recreation activities are financed by credit," summarized one casino official.[30] New Jersey and Las Vegas make generous provision for gaming on the cuff. The one exception is New Jersey's treating of gambling debts as a legal obligation, a situation that does not hold in Nevada. In New Jersey, nearly all of the state's receipts from the casinos are a function of gross win, after bad debts are deducted. The state, therefore, uses its powers to help serve as a collection agency for the casinos.

Atlantic City's casinos approved $588 million in credit slips in 1980. There is enormous variation in credit practices, depending upon the merchandising approach of the casino. Those that specialize in high rollers tend to provide more liberal credit; those that try to attract the general public feel under less of an obligation. In June 1981, for example, credit play ranged from 15 percent of the drop at Harrah's to 41 percent at Caesar's.

According to the Casino Control Commission, more than $437 million in credit markers were redeemed by patrons before they left the casino in 1980. An additional $108 million was collected when markers were deposited in the patron's banking accounts. No less than $33 million worth of markers bounced, despite a number of credit requirements embodied in the casino enabling statute, as well as the administrative law that has grown up around their operations.[31] Casino credit applicants are required by law to supply their home addresses, employer, and checking-account information to casino officials. The casino is supposed to verify this information. By state law, markers have to be deposited in the gambler's personal checking account within seven days if less than $1000; within 90 days if more than $2000. This has not prevented bad debts.

Either because of the necessities of competition, or the legal status of debt collection, New Jersey casinos have been more generous in extending credit than their western peers. A projection of a model Nevada casino in 1975 was done by the National Commission on Gambling with the cooperation of casino operators. About one third of all projected gaming transactions involved some form of credit, with approximately 3 percent of all credit extended by the casinos resulting in a bad debt. Nevada casinos have roughly a 1 percent bad-debt figure in terms of total gross win; New Jersey casinos have currently doubled that amount.

The years are different and gambler behavior may have changed with them, but, at least according to *Rouge et Noir*, the "liberal credit policies of some of the Atlantic City casinos serve to burn out customers who had trouble dealing with the ready availability of table credit." The magazine suggests that Nevada's casinos were experiencing an increase in uncollectible casino receipts as "gamblers in financial trouble tried unsuccessfully to solve their difficulty at Nevada tables."[32]

New Jersey has calmly acquiesced in fostering a level of credit that has generated substantial debt losses despite legal enforceability. The state permits the casinos a provision of up to 4 percent of gross win for bad debts. Assuming that only half of the sums gambled in a casino are cash, this indicates an 8 percent effective bad-debt ratio on credit transactions. Even a small proportion of this can amount to a lot of money. The opportunities for blatant fraud need not be imagined; experience confirms them. It has been reported, for example, that the relatively low win ratio for table games in Atlantic City stems from credit players taking down their entire line at the beginning, playing only a little, and walking out. "In effect they have received an interest free loan." According to some financial analysts, this stems from bad management and poor controls, but the possibilities for connivance here are all too obvious.[33]

Scams against casinos are not unique to New Jersey. A recent major credit fraud against Resorts Paradise Hotel in the Bahamas amounted to $400,000. The possibilities of collusion in similar instances, with false credit references used with the cooperation of casino personnel, are evident, particularly given the sloppiness of enforcing credit-application requirements as well as their sheer scale.[34]

In the hearings on the licensing of Caesars, for example, evidence was produced by the New Jersey Division of Gaming Enforcement that the casino operators had given credit extremely loosely. At least ninety individuals of criminal background had received substantial amounts of credit, with most of the credit infor-

information nominally called for on the forms simply omitted. There was a 43 percent writeoff for noncollection of the credit given to these individuals in violation of the casino's normal credit procedures.[35] It does not take a fan of gangster films to appreciate the possibilities of the casinos serving as illicit cash conduits for loans or payoffs through the casual granting of credit.

The Varieties of Skimming

The nature of the entertainment business, combined with the abundance of cash flowing through a casino, provides a fertile ground for other types of illegal ploys. There are almost an infinite number of ways to divert funds or services in a large casino hotel. One of the more common practices is the simple noncharging of guests for accommodations and services. While some courtesies are often extended to the big spender at normal hotels, the basic income of the latter depends on direct collections for services rendered. In the case of a casino hotel, the pattern of providing full or partial "complimentaries" in return for the expectation that the recipient will lose worthwhile sums at the tables has long been a substantial part of the business. There is no effective way to control it.

The National Commission on Gambling in its projection of a model casino suggested that about 15 percent of the typical operating budget was expended on the provision of complimentary rooms, drinks, food, entertainment, and air transportation to its preferred customers.[36] But this projection masks an enormous variation in individual operating approaches. For example, the major Las Vegas casinos have had complimentary expenditures varying from a meager 8.2 percent of total hotel revenues and services in 1977 at the Showboat to 45 percent at the Dunes.

In an analysis of operating statistics of publicly owned Nevada casinos published by *Forbes Magazine* in 1978, a reasonably consistent trend was indicated of around 25 percent of total hotel revenues going as free services, while markers as a percentage of casino revenues were anywhere from a low of 1.7 percent at the

Golden Nugget in downtown Las Vegas to a high of 42 percent at the Del Webb Corporation.[37] The junket, or full expense-paid package for heavy rollers, is the height of the art form. The casino product is relatively nondifferentiated, with the take at the various types of games set by a combination of regulatory strictures or market competition. The complimentaries and entertainment are the differentiating elements within a competitive market, and these are the most difficult elements to control.

The possibilities of filtering off some of the casinos' take to a favorite few – licitly or illicitly – are great, and the amounts involved are far from trivial.[38] In 1980, Atlantic City's casino hotels were reportedly giving away $71 million worth of free drinks, meals, rooms, and show tickets to gamblers, and this was in addition to more than a half billion dollars extended on credit (a quarter of the $2.3 billion of chips purchased by gamblers in 1980 were bought on credit).[39] In the first six months of 1982, the Golden Nugget alone issued $68 million in credit and $17.5 million in complimentaries.[40] These figures represent the "legitimate" pressure of doing business. To them must be added the possibilities of outright diversion of casino funds in order to avoid taxes and possibly to serve as payoffs or as a "bank" for illegitimate purposes.

The track record of illegal activity in this area is substantial. *Rouge et Noir*, for example, cites a report dated January 17, 1977, by Dennis C. Gomes, then chief of the Nevada Gaming Control Board, which alleges that a raid conducted by its audit division in May 1976 uncovered an embezzlement on the order of $7 million from the Stardust Hotel in Las Vegas. The same publication cites a number of lesser but still significant frauds. Moreover, the cases typically publicized are those representing some form of fraud perpetrated against the casinos. Those involving collusion may not be uncommon, but are seldom brought to light.[41]

Atlantic City has instituted procedures to avoid outright skimming. Just how successful these have been remains to be seen. A statement made in the course of a recent interview with one of the former Casino Control commissioners summarizes some of the doubts: "We are doing everything we can think of to prevent it – I'm still not sure it's not taking place."[42]

Abscam

When gambling was legalized, the fear of corruption could only be appeased by a continuous verbal barrage from the state house indicating the broad variety of safeguards being implemented. To a chorus of groans from the casinos, a $30 million a year investigatory and administrative framework evolved to scrutinize in great detail all casino employees, down to the lowliest croupier in training. Commissioners and other state officials traveled abroad as well as to Nevada, returning with reassuring statements on how much they had learned and how their education would be reflected in the impenetrable barriers to be established for governing the Atlantic City tiger.

When Robert R. Ferguson, chairman and chief executive officer of the First National State Bank of New Jersey, the state's largest bank, was testifying on the adequacy of these measures, he reflected the establishment view: "I think you have to face the organized crime issue head on when you talk about financing casinos . . . [We] have demonstrated in Atlantic City that organized crime can be kept out of casino operations. The strong control commission, like New Jersey's, will discover participation by organized crime very quickly and correct any problem that arises."[43]

A few months after this testimony, Americans in every state were watching video tapes of New Jersey's senior senator, Harrison Williams, as he boasted in an October 1979 meeting that the head of the Casino Control Commission was "his man." He claimed responsibility for a favorable ruling for Ritz Associates, permitting them to reconstruct an old hotel in Atlantic City rather than requiring them to build a completely new one, a savings of some $30 million. Williams' wife at the time was a paid consultant to Hardwick Companies, which held the majority interest in Ritz Associates. (It should be noted that Hardwick was proposing a boardwalk hotel costing approximately $100 million, involving renovation and new construction to yield 540 rooms with a 35,000-square-foot casino.) Williams' codefendant and political confidant and fundraiser, Alexander Feinberg, was seen on the same video tape bragging that he asked the commission's vice-president, Kenneth McDonald, to get help for Ritz Associates after he was called by Mrs. Williams on behalf of the developer. "McDonald and Lordi happened to talk. He [Williams] talked to Lordi and I talked to McDonald."[44]

The Abscam investigation was national in scope. The New Jersey revelations revolved around casino activity. An FBI agent named Amoroso posed as an emissary of an Arab sheik anxious to get involved in the casino business. He met several times with Richard Coffee, New Jersey Democratic chairman, in an effort to expedite state permits for a check-cashing business that the sheik proposed to establish in a number of New Jersey cities. A bribe of $50,000 was proposed in order to secure Coffee's goodwill in facilitating this activity. "Coffee clearly understood from Amoroso that the Sheik wanted the check-cashing sources to launder the sources of money skimmed from the casinos."[45] According to one published account, Coffee promised to use his influence with the state banking commissioner to deliver the appropriate licenses.[46]

The mayor of Camden, Angelo Errichetti, a long-time southern New Jersey political power, enthusiastically acted as the contact man between the supposed sheik and the politicians, as well as for McDonald of the Casino Control Commission. It is interesting to note that, in an effort to reassure Errichetti of their bonafide intentions, the FBI group deposited a million dollars in an Atlantic City bank that Errichetti had been touting for months. The mayor claimed that Steven Perskie, the state senator who structured casino gambling in New Jersey, had an interest in the bank.[47] Deposits to assure the goodwill of bankers is not very different from normal business activity and political involvement, but it indicates the potential power of the casinos in terms of deposit capabilities.

There were repeated assertions in the course of the taped meetings held with both Errichetti and George Katz (a close associate of Senator Williams) of connections with Lansky, and specifically with Alvin Malnik, who was involved with Caesars World and the Teamsters' Pension Fund. In addition, Mayor Errichetti stated that Jerry Catena, who has been described as the boss of the old Genovese crime family, owned Joseph Lordi, chairman of the Casino Control Commission. The same assertion was made by Tony Torcasio, who had been hired to run the proposed Penthouse Casino. Torcasio described in substantial detail the ways he could skim huge sums of money from the casino without the owners, much less the IRS, being aware of it.[48]

Both Errichetti and Katz claimed that the Perlmans of Caesars World still had close ties with Lansky and Malnik. Errichetti had a contact who would speak to Lansky in order to assure his friendly attitude toward the proposed investment by the sheik in Atlantic City casinos. Howard Criden, alleged to have been a close associate of the Lansky group as well as a business partner of Malnik in several Florida deals, was brought onto the scene. It was Criden who delivered a number of congressmen. Criden was taped reporting that he had lunched with Lansky and that Lansky would work with the sheik. Furthermore, Lansky had sent Criden to Malnik to arrange for appropriate land transactions in Atlantic City.

Lansky, said Criden, was already involved in Atlantic City through Caesars Palace and the Boardwalk Regency, with Malnik acting as the go-between for the Perlman interests and Lansky. Criden further suggested that Resorts International was party in some measure to an affiliation with Lansky.[49] Federal prosecutors said that a $100,000 bribe intended for McDonald was passed in early 1979 to Mayor Errichetti. Moreover, Senator Williams convinced the sheik to provide $20 million in financing for Hardwick, based on assurances that there would be no legal problems. Senator Williams secured a $1 million commission for his effort.[50]

The state's ability to handle its own can of worms was further cast into doubt when the Abscam probe was transferred from New Jersey to Brooklyn. Some evidence suggests that old political friendships in the Garden State might have been responsible for the leaks that brought Abscam to a halt and inhibited the possibilities of prosecution based upon its results. It should be noted that, while a number of the participants have been tried and found guilty of charges based on the sting operation, Lordi, chairman of the Casino Control Commission, vehemently denied any political bending described by those who claimed to control

him. It is very difficult to draw a line between phony name drop-
ping and hints of political muscle while watching the tapes or
reading the transcript of the Abscam investigation. As promise
after promise is made to deliver the goods in Atlantic City,
whether licenses or zoning changes, the sheer scale of the assurances raises some doubt as to their validity.

Certainly, however, the greed of leading New Jersey politicians
came through loud and clear. Mayor Errichetti of Camden obviously had a very close relationship with the vice-chairman of the
Casino Control Commission as well as the chairman of the New
Jersey Democratic Committee. Whether the influence he claimed
was part of an effort to secure money strictly for himself, or
whether he acted as a conduit for graft, or whether he could do so
on the scale that he suggested, is still open to question. Again and
again in the course of the meetings, the emphasis on Errichetti's
capacity to deliver not merely casino locations but also licenses is
strenuously made. Errichetti referred to himself as "their bag
man," claiming the capacity to deliver four out of five commissioners for $100,000. This may merely have been Errichetti's at-
tempt to pocket some money, but he was able to deliver the
seemingly receptive vice-chairman of the commission in person.

After the smoke of Abscam cleared, the results were surprisingly minimal, though a number of the politicians either went to
jail or ended their political careers. The Casino Control Commission was replaced with full-time members (see Chapter 4). After
some horse trading, the commission's chairman, Joseph Lordi,
continued in that role until his retirement the following summer.
The viewpoint of Atlantic City's business and political leaders was
expressed in the course of an interview on the governor's reaction: "Governor Byrne wanted to be Attorney General [of the
U.S.]. He panicked when the Abscam investigation mentioned a
commission member. He replaced the whole commission and
tried to get rid of Lordi – he scared the investors away – [we lost]
months of time in terms of licensing."[51]

Abscam probably limited the advance of gambling in other
states. The revelations gave pause to New York, Pennsylvania,
Connecticut, and Massachusetts.

Political Pressures and Responses

The process of licensing, the level of dependency on procedures that are open to judgment, evokes a hunger for certification. A casino hotel with an initial cost of several hundred million dollars, yielding a net of $60 million a year before debt payments and depreciation charges, can become a simple hotel, badly placed in an archaic resort town, by a slip of licensing.

The availability of financial resources to construct a casino depends on the assurance of statutory success. Casino developers have three alternative approaches to guarantee success: having enough wealth or collateral outside the Atlantic City development itself (as in the case of Bally's or Resorts), finding someone interested in a high-risk loan, or taking out insurance through a political contact to assure potential investors that there will be no problems. In the course of the Abscam findings, this last approach comes up again and again as the professional confidence man employed by the FBI continuously states, in one form or another, "If you can show me that you've got the juice, we'll back you up in Atlantic City."[52]

Regulation and disastrous penalties for their violation can lead either to the exclusion of all but the purest of pure backgrounds and operations, which is the theory behind the punitive rules of the game, or to an effort to secure insurance licitly or otherwise. All of this takes place within a state of general fear that a flattening out of the Atlantic City casino phenomenon will cause potential newcomers to avoid the troubled area. This last element creates a pressure for letting down the bars. The pure – or fearless – may be too few. If other regions start bidding for casinos, their attraction may be not only their markets but also their willingness to cooperate.

Is it possible to have casino gaming and appropriate regulation, with none of the going-ons so dramatically and painfully brought to public attention by Abscam? The new penalties invoked against the Del Webb Corporation and against the Perlman brothers may signal the end of the old order of casino operations, or it may be merely a temporary wrinkle in the way things always have been.

At this stage of the game, conclusions must be tentative. But the track record of casinos in Atlantic City provides some insight.

The casinos are enormously costly to build and equip, making them extremely vulnerable to pressures of delay during the construction period. There are vast opportunities and incentives for front-end skimming, of loading up construction costs, which have varied by a staggering 300 percent from the Golden Nugget to the Tropicana, and pocketing the proceeds. In addition, the process of buying labor peace is far from unique to Atlantic City, but the penalties for not doing so may be, given the dubious character of some of the local unions.

Once open for business, the stringency of the regulatory mechanisms and the requirement for annual relicensing, though calculated to create a clean management, also impose the need to make sure of strong political backing. The casinos do not have to give bribes directly; an enterprise purchasing millions of dollars in services and goods a year may learn to do business with vendors who have "friends." This practice is accentuated by the casinos' vulnerability to the very regulatory mechanisms that are supposed to keep them clean.

The casinos are not like other businesses. Their enterprise embodies not only large amounts of ready cash but also complimentaries given with a lavish hand. The Boeing Aircraft Company can be criticized for maintaining a hunting lodge to entertain buyers of airplanes, but this is trivial when viewed within the context of casino operating procedures, which entail free favors and credit as standard operating procedures. The more obvious sinners of the past can be chased from the Temple, as the Perlmans were. We would seriously question, however, whether a new generation of more sophisticated newcomers, with perhaps equally close gangland ties, can be avoided.

LEARNING FROM ATLANTIC CITY

New York, Pennsylvania, and the numerous other communities contemplating legalization must examine more than the Atlantic City balance sheet. They must take into account the estimated size of the total gambling market in the United States. There is a limit to the amount Americans will spend on gambling, and communities that expect economic gains comparable with those achieved in Atlantic City and Nevada may merely end up with a share of a market that may now be close to its upper limit. Moreover, communities must consider whether the profits from the casinos will be the result of a shifting of money from the other forms of legal gambling – racetracks or lotteries – that are now a source of state income. But the result of legalization in need of the most careful consideration may be the social cost of state-approved gambling – its effects on crime, morality, and the public good.

The Atlantic City Balance Sheet

Atlantic City is still evolving as a gambling center. The specifics of the environment, the peculiar historical foundations upon which the casinos were built, and the poor socioeconomic conditions of the city and its surrounding region to a large extent define what has happened and what will happen in Atlantic City. While these idiosyncrasies must be kept in mind, other localities interested in the potential of casino gaming can learn much from New Jersey's adoption of gambling as a tool for economic revitalization. Atlantic City's track record, while good in many respects, is far from perfect. Each of the major positive developments has brought with it negative developments.

Positive. There has been a massive increase in taxable property wealth. The requirement that the casinos be accompanied by new (and, earlier, substantially rehabilitated) 500-room-minimum hotel facilities has vastly expanded the taxable assessment base of the community. The nine casino hotels in Atlantic City are currently assessed at more than $831 million – more than half the total for the entire community. The casinos in 1982 paid approximately $37 million in real-property taxes to the city.

Negative. A hurricane of land speculation attended the acceptance of casinos, bringing in its wake an upward sweep in real-estate values. In turn, this entailed serious displacement not only among the poor but also among homeowners who did not wish to sell their property but now encountered onerous tax burdens. The bidding up of property values, and with them rents, has driven other forms of commerce from the community, leaving in its wake a desolate stretch of abandoned retailing and other older facilities. While Atlantic City has enjoyed an increase in tax revenues, it has also seen increases in municipal expenditures directly related to casino activities; the long-term requirements made of the community, as its infrastructure becomes stretched to the breaking point, have yet to be faced.

Positive. The state's take, at 8 percent of the gross win after allowance for bad debts, yielded more than $100 million in 1982.

Negative. The state's essentially free ride in securing revenue from the casinos may become increasingly bumpy. The promises made in the course of the campaign to legalize the casinos, in terms of new programs and new dollars for the elderly, have largely been ignored, but they remain a continuous political irritant. The state must begin to defend its casino-derived income, investing significant amounts in and around Atlantic City. Moreover, there lurks the issue of upgrading Atlantic City to meet the challenge of new gaming locations. The state is now expected to support drastically needed housing reinvestment within the city. The nominal yield to the state currently is more a measure of the state's avoidance of responsibility than it is of a truly "free" new source of revenue.

Positive. The casinos have directly generated 30,000 jobs.

Negative. The bulk of the job growth within the city is in the hands of suburbanites, and the massive job increase within the casinos has not been accompanied by equally vigorous growth in noncasino employment. Instead, the reverse seems to be the case. Despite vigorous efforts (particularly in minority hiring), the basic core of the unemployed and welfare recipients of the city has not been significantly diminished by the advent of the casinos.

The Future Gambling Market

States now contemplating legalization cannot base their estimates of profit solely on the Atlantic City experience, even if they decide that the balance sheet, in spite of the negative side, is favorable. In our estimation, there are limits to the number of gambling dollars that will be spent within the United States. Atlantic City, at the very least, is blunting Nevada's rate of growth. Casino gaming is also funneling funds from other forms of legitimate wagering. The state revenues derived from the casinos must be viewed in the context of some diminution of the take from the racetracks.

We would suggest that the legalization of major casino facilities elsewhere in the continental United States will represent only in decreasing proportions "new money" flowing onto the nation's gaming tables; most new casino facilities will draw money at the expense of existing gaming facilities in Atlantic City or Nevada. *The future market for casino gaming will be more a division of the amount currently spent on all forms of gambling than it will be an expansion.* Las Vegas and Atlantic City already show signs of competing for the same market. The issue of whether the Atlantic City casinos are nearing peak volume is an incessant question both for present and prospective casino operators and developers. There is probably no more closely observed index than that of the monthly gross win figures that emerge from the nation's two prime gaming localities.

Casino hotels are enormously expensive to build, to operate, and to finance. While much of the investment community's turmoil reflects the horrendous cost overruns, inadequacies of the management of the casinos, and possibly skimming and payoffs through inflated capital costs, the question of market size and profitability can be tested by studying the Atlantic City facilities.

Some Measures of Casino Profitability

Definitive statements about any element of casino gaming are difficult to find, especially statements about profitability and return on investment. There are vagaries of individual management strategies and variations in capital and start-up costs in this relatively new arena – some legitimate, some the result of incompetence, and some possibly the result of less innocent realities. The dramatic increases in the costs of capital, particularly at the height of casino development fervor, hang over them all.

The casino operators repeatedly told New Jersey's Casino Control Commission and the state legislature in 1982 that a number of facilities *at the very least* were running in or close to the red. New investment has been hindered, and the casinos maintained that only major changes in regulatory requirements could alleviate the financial bind. These complaints have been well publicized and are now part of the accepted wisdom; the result has been attempts by the governing agencies to ease the casinos' way to greater profits.

Assuming good management and appropriate capital and operating costs, a simple model of what casino profitability in Atlantic City should be is the key to understanding the market.

1. *Capital costs*. The capital costs required in constructing a casino vary enormously. While the Casino Control Commission has
made heroic efforts to standardize accounting procedures, the issue of the real costs involved in construction have defied the best
of accounting techniques.

On the one hand, there is the situation of Resorts International,
which was permitted to refurbish an extant facility, able to buy
land very cheaply, and open with a minimum of "front-end"
stress. If the costs of the land it purchased for future development
are removed from the announced capital costs involved, its open-
ing-day figure was certainly under the $50 million mark. On the
other hand, there is the sad case of Bally's, which attempted to
build using a fast-track approach, with a substantial part of the de-
sign incomplete while construction was under way. A continuous
flow of structural changes, incredible amounts of overtime, and
the like, resulted in reported costs of nearly $300 million. It is in-
teresting to observe that the original projections for Bally's involved costs under the $100 million mark. As late as August
1979, it was estimated at $176 million; the reality was an addi-
tional $100 million over that figure.[1] The Tropicana Casino Ho-
tel, built under the aegis of the Ramada Corporation, was forecast
to come in at $130 million and instead cost $330 million.[2] By
way of contrast, the Golden Nugget, only slightly smaller than the
two latter establishments, had cost approximately $100 million by
opening day.

Rather than getting lost in the intricacies of individual casino
developments, it is better to deal with reasonably estimated model
numbers. The current cost of building a major city hotel, even in
such difficult environments as New York City and San Francisco,
is approximately $100,000 per room, including the usual match-
ing provisions for dining facilities, conference rooms, and so
forth. In terms of rehabilitation, the Commodore Hotel next to
New York City's Grand Central Station, facing out on busy Forty-
Second Street, was stripped to its iron work and completely re-
built to luxury standards for approximately $75,000 per room.

Assuming that Atlantic City's construction costs at worst should
be no more than New York City's, the typical 500-room casino
hotel could have its noncasino facilities built for little more than

$50 million dollars. The casino itself tends to be about 40,000 square feet, with some exceptions on both sides of this figure. The precise cost of the casino and its fixtures will depend on the arrangements made to secure the equipment, but for the moment it is appropriate to assume that the total of the casino and its facilities should be available for less than $50 million (allowing an excess of $1000 per square foot). This would yield a total cost of approximately $100 million for a casino hotel complex.

Assume further that these estimates are somewhat optimistic. There is a requirement for working capital, preopening expenses, financing of the lag during training and construction, and so forth. Another $50 million must be added to cover these miscellaneous elements. This would produce a very rough model capital cost of $150 million. Given the nine casino hotels open in Atlantic City at the beginning of 1982, *appropriate* capital costs would be in the neighborhood of $1.35 billion.[3]

2. *Operating costs*. What is the level of gross win required to operate our model Atlantic City casino hotel before facing up to funded debt and equity requirements as well as depreciation? Again, these elements have significant variation depending, for example, on the configurations of the several hotels and management policy in terms of services provided.

Operating-cost estimates of the individual casinos have been undertaken by *Rouge et Noir*. The average of these individual estimates is approximately $10 million per month ($10 million of the win is required to take care of operating costs).[4] The projected casino hotel would require $120 million a year to cover its operating costs; the sum total of the nine hotels' operating costs would be approximately $1.080 billion.

3. *Gross win*. The gross win of the casinos (the difference between the amounts wagered by and the winnings of the gamblers) is subject to the operational competence of the individual casinos and the rules of the game. In the case of a large casino, for example, elimination of the early-surrender option in blackjack may mean as much as an additional $10 million win per year. Changes in the regulation governing the number of modest-bet tables initially required of the casinos represent a potential nearly double this. The area of twenty-four-hour operation is somewhat

controversial, but at least one gaming authority suggests that it might well yield nearly as much as the change in the rules governing blackjack.[5]

There is a long break-in period for a new casino. The general feeling is that peak volumes are not reached until after a year's seasoning. This is not unique to casinos; major regional shopping centers do not reach their peak until they have been open for three business years.[6] Gas shortages, credit crunches, and all the elements of general business conditions obviously play a role. Within these vagaries, the market reality of a gross win of $1.4 billion in 1982 speaks for itself and confirms the market's forecast of success.[7]

4. *Net operating profit.* The gross win estimates of $1.4 billion (less the state take of 8 percent, or $112 million) and operating costs of $1.080 billion would yield approximately $200 million to service debt, reward equity investors, and cope with depreciation. The tentative nature of these estimates must be stressed. They are based on appropriately realistic capital costs. Future estimates of gross win must be viewed with the same trepidation extended to any future projection of gross sales by any retail establishment. But the figures do seem reasonably accurate, based upon the historical productivity of the several casinos. The same strictures hold for the data on operating costs presented here, even though operating costs are particularly subject to the uncertainties of inflationary pressures.

5. *Return on investment.* The data imputed above with a net operating yield of $200 million based on total investment of $1.35 billion suggest a contribution to debt, depreciation, and profit (net operating income) of approximately 15 percent (for the moment forgetting allowance for aging of facilities), or a total return of capital in slightly more than six years.

If the gross win estimates for 1983 prove to be realistic, even assuming inflationary increases in operating costs of 10 percent, the casinos would secure net operating income of roughly 33 percent – $1.8 billion, less the state's $144 million and operating expenses of $1.2 billion, leaves $456 million, or 33 percent of the capital costs of $1.35 billion. It should further be noted that no new casinos over and above the nine projected should be operational until the end of 1983 at the earliest. The casino return on investment figure is competitive with even the top quartile of American industry and compares positively with Las Vegas.

The Securities and Exchange Commission filing by Bally's Park Place for the nine months that ended September 30, 1980, together with its gross win data for the subsequent three months ending December 31, 1980, provides an independent check on the estimates above. In the first nine months of the year, Bally's achieved total revenue of $157.3 million. Costs and expenses, including bad debts, were $107.7 million, leaving a contribution to debt, depreciation, and profit of just under $50 million in nine months. This period did include some start-up costs (the casino opening in December of 1979), as well as a very slow yield in the break-in months of January and February. The three months after the close of the filing date, from September through December 1980, yielded the casino a volume of $35 million, roughly proportionate to the prior nine months.

Bally's total contribution to debt, depreciation, and profit for its first year of operation was approximately $65 million (the $49.6 million recorded in the first nine months annualized in a conservative fashion based on the fact that the casino volume was at least in accord with the earlier part of the year). For the $150 million model projected cost, this would be a very respectable return on investment of around 43 percent before depreciation. But Bally's capital costs were nearly double the model's imputed figure. In this regard, one experienced investment adviser suggested, in a 128-page study of gaming stocks, that the financial climate in Atlantic City is far rosier than some casino executives have let on.[8] Still this does not mean that the business is readily expandable.

Total Casino Potential

Communities contemplating legalization of casinos must try to determine whether Atlantic City represents the equivalent of a preemptive strike, a gathering together of a critical mass that so dominates the casino market as to limit the potential of other locations. Those who may wish to invest in casinos in Atlantic City must decide whether the present assemblage of nine casinos depicts a topping out of the market. To Atlantic City, as well as New Jersey and the Casino Control Commission, the issue of whether there is a volume potential adequate to sustain significant additions to the present casino hotel array becomes ever more pressing.

The impact of the Meadowlands Race Track in New Jersey on its neighbors is a chastening example on the negative side. The new super facilities in the Meadowlands have caused an abrupt shrinkage in competitive facilities within a broad commuting radius, evidence that the pool of legitimate gambling and racing is quite sharply defined. The question is whether this holds true for gaming.

Precise answers to the questions above are impossible. Great Britain's casinos offer an interesting comparison. In 1978, there were 125 casinos and 15,000 betting shops. Between 1972 and 1976, the handle for the industry (the amount bet) grew at an annual rate in excess of 30 percent. This took place while the British economy as a whole was moribund. The win from casinos and slot machines in Great Britain was 0.18 percent of the gross national product in 1976. The U.S. equivalent at that time was 0.07 percent of GNP. If U.S. casino and slot-machine wins in 1976 had been 0.18 percent of GNP, the win for the casinos would have been $3.4 billion as opposed to the actual $1.1 billion.[9] If Great Britain's incidence figure is extended to the current U.S. GNP, now slightly in excess of $2.9 trillion, the result would suggest a potential of $5.7 billion.

The experience of Great Britain is not necessarily a good analogue. It is distorted by variance in custom, levels of disposable income, and, not least, the enormous flow of high-rolling Middle East money upon which the 1976 win data are predicated. If we were to assume that, given the far higher level of per capita disposable income available in the United States, this nominal figure could be increased by one half, it would yield under $8 billion in 1983 dollars. Recent estimates for the United States tend to parallel this projection.[10]

But even these relatively optimistic data indicate that the peak of available volume has been reached, unless there is a shift to a much greater proportion of total consumer spending on casino gaming. The present facilities of Atlantic City and Nevada, in terms of current dollars, are absorbing about 60 percent of the potential based upon this projected share of GNP. Plans afoot for new casinos in Atlantic City will increase capacity by nearly half, while Las Vegas is painfully coping with the overexpansion of the last two years. So the possibilities of creating an equivalent of Atlantic City in another area seem marginal at best.

This analysis does not preclude smaller facilities in regions that have immediate high potential or heavy traffic, such as some of the proposed casino resorts in the Poconos or Catskills or, for that matter, the kind of small casinos that exist throughout the Caribbean and Europe. But these are relatively modest revenue producers, items added to resort areas rather than dynamos of urban revitalization. More major groups of casino hotels that would rival Atlantic City's portion of the national gaming take are probably not feasible. New facilities must increasingly compete for the market share with those already on the scene. A new Atlantic City can only be supported by feasting off the old. For example, while some of Nevada's problems are accentuated by the immediacies of the recession and Mexico's devaluated currency, it is evident that many of them stem from Atlantic City competition.

The amount people spend on all forms of gambling combined is not limitless. The extension of casino gambling may be beginning to push other revenue-producing "activities of chance" to the wall. No less an authority than leisure-market entrepreneur Sonny Werblin points to the fact that "the history of all race tracks vis-à-vis casinos, is that the tracks go out of business very quickly."[11] He further suggests that New York State is losing legal gaming business to Atlantic City, which cannot be continued too much longer. Atlantic City has preempted the market and, from a regional perspective, is skimming from other forms of gaming.

The New York Racing Association has been a strong supporter of the anticasino interests in New York, for obvious reasons. In the words of James P. Heffnan, president of the New York Association: "This year [1980] New York State solely from the New York Racing Association operation on-track will receive more than $60 million in revenue – and will pay in real estate taxes a total of $8 million." Heffnan pointed out that in 1979, in New York and Connecticut, the total on- and off-track betting on horse racing was approximately $1.8 billion. (It is interesting to note that $282 million in 1979 was bet at the approximately 200 betting shops in the metropolitan New York area.) The Meadowlands, at the same time, had a total handle of $582 million, including harness racing. The total metropolitan bet in 1979, on all forms of horse races, was $2.8 billion. The zero-sum potential of incorporating casinos within this context is illustrated by studies at various New York metropolitan tracks, which indicate that from 30 to 60 percent of those currently attending and betting on horse races patronize casinos. At least in Heffnan's view, "There can be no doubt that if casino gaming is permitted in metropolitan New York, it will account for a substantial loss in wagering on thoroughbred harness racing both on- and off-track."[12] And certainly the current problems facing New York's OTB should be seen as an omen for the future.

Despite Atlantic City's gaming draw, it too is highly vulnerable to competition. New York's legalization of casino gaming would have a severe impact. The current estimates, and they can be no more than just that, suggest a decline on the order of a third in total volume.[13] A case can be made that the present Atlantic City infrastructure is so bereft of any pulling power other than the casinos that without significant improvements, not least of them a major convention center, there could well be a much greater market penetration and resulting volume loss. A substantial reinvestment of the revenues from gaming is necessary to counteract this.

Who Pays?

Las Vegas is ringed by a hundred miles of desert. Atlantic City sits in an area encompassing well over 20 million people. The merchandising mix of the two rivals reflects this difference. The same games are available in New Jersey and the major casino hotels of Las Vegas. The action, however, is vastly different.

While blackjack as a proportion of total win is roughly comparable (approximately 30 percent), baccarat and craps are far less significant in the Garden State. But the major difference is in revenue derived from the slot machines. In Nevada the casino hotels essentially pull from a national, if not international, market, emphasizing heavy rollers to whom the slots represent low-class amateurism. In Nevada casino complexes with gaming revenues of $20 million or more, slot machines contribute under 30 percent. (The slots, on the other hand, are present everywhere else in Las Vegas and Reno, so that the total state take from them is much higher than holds true in the major casino hotels.) In New Jersey, revenues derived from the slot machines are pushing close to the halfway mark.[14]

A strong case may be made that in New Jersey the hotel part of the casinos is largely a tribute to the state requirements more than an integral element in the casino operation. The hotels are costly *symbols of failure* to achieve real economic revitalization of Atlantic City as a resort. Occupancy figures are relatively low, even though inflated by very generous complimentary use. For better or worse, Atlantic City's casino action, the state take, and the city's revitalized job base are largely a tribute to small-scale lower-income gamers. The tables in the casinos may provide an image of James Bond and Monte Carlo; the real dollars are in the one-arm bandits. Table 24 summarizes data for table games versus revenues for coin-operated devices in New Jersey's casinos for July 1981, indicating the significance of the latter. Within the domain of coin-operated devices, the 5-cent and 25-cent slot machines are clearly favored. In fact, the one sector of the national market that seems to be expandable lies in the area of decentralized slot machines, which, however, is the most regressive and least "export-oriented" segment of the market. It would truly be a punitive form of locally harmful taxation of the poor and youthful unwary.

Most characteristic of Atlantic City's gamers are the bus people. Seemingly endless streams of charter buses bring in the raw material of the casinos' gross win. In 1982, nearly nine million visitors were carried on the 300,000 bustrips counted by the Atlantic County Transportation Authority.[15] Lip service is given to the cause of the high roller, and, in the case of the Playboy facility, a total orientation toward the big-stakes gambler was projected and advertised. The reality is that, after a very brief test, Playboy also went into a major bus-promotion campaign.

According to Steve Norton, the executive vice-president of Resorts International, the bus people are individuals losing somewhere around $20 to $30 per person each day. The casino cost to bus them in and provide them with a lunch is running about $6-$10 per head, leaving a net of close to $15-$20. The economics of the bus business are straightforward: forty people to a bus with a net win of $20 per head will yield $800 per busload.[16]

No detailed field survey of the origins of Atlantic City's gamers has been undertaken, much less one weighted by level of loss. Current observers tend to agree that roughly 85 percent of the total traffic, if not the total dollars gambled, originates in a relatively even split between the greater New York, Philadelphia, and New Jersey areas. An additional 7 or 8 percent come from Baltimore/Washington, with the rest from a variety of other locations. According to one seasoned observer, "These typically are middle class people, the bulk of them coming out of cash businesses, small retailing, etc., and they bring their cash down here."[17] About 30 percent of the bus traffic in this one estimation are elderly individuals who cannot afford to lose but persist in doing so.

Judging from the hotel occupancy rates, which dwindle to not much more than a 40 percent occupancy level in the depths of the winter season, it is the daytripper who is dominant in Atlantic City. This contrasts substantially to the situation in Las Vegas, where a typical visitor spends 3.8 days.

Even in Las Vegas, despite the costs of getting there, most of the traffic is represented by individuals with relatively modest incomes. Roughly a third of the 1976-77 visitors, for example, had total family incomes under $25,000, with an additional third with incomes around $25,000 to $30,000. The Las Vegas gambler income level is raised by the prominence of the town as a convention center. Those who arrive by bus tend to have very low incomes, with 41 percent at less than $10,000 and an additional 33 percent at the $10,000 to $15,000 level. Slice off the convention attendees and those who arrive by air, and the modest means of the Las Vegas gamer is not much different from that of the gamer in Atlantic City.[18]

Every study of casino gaming has indicated its regressive nature. The National Commission on Gambling has summarized the situation neatly. One of the major findings of its 1976 survey was that the expenditures in gambling were regressive, that is, that lower-income groups spent a greater percentage of their income on gambling than other income groups. This was true for gambling expenditures taken as a whole as it was for individual games. So taxes on legal gambling are regressive; people of modest income end up paying for most of Atlantic City's glitter.[19]

The lure of the casinos is most powerful among those who are least experienced in calculating the real odds. Underage gamblers are a major problem. One study of Atlantic City high school students, for example, found that 72 percent of the students gamble in casinos, with approximately a quarter of the total admitting that they gamble often.[20] During May, June, and July 1981, the casinos turned away more than 41,000 minors at their doors, while another 10,000 youngsters under eighteen had to be escorted off the floor. Despite all the efforts of the Casino Control Commission, there seems little that can be done to prevent minors from gambling.[21]

Atlantic City, unlike Las Vegas, is much more of a homegrown market, and thus more like other prospective sites that must draw on local patronage. So the question raised in a review of Connecticut's gaming by one observer seems pertinent to other areas investigating the profitability of casinos. With regard to overall state revenues, "there has been no economic analysis of the distortions generated in state and local government's economy by the automatic loss of hundreds of millions of dollars by those who wager. The ironic truth may be that when all is said and done, Connecticut and other states are subsidizing the gaming industry and professional gamblers – and consequently are exporting more dollars than they are receiving in revenue."[22]

The report of the National Commission on Gambling indicates that widespread availability of legal gambling increases the gambling population. The rate of participation in illegal gambling in states that have some form of legalized gambling is far greater than it is in areas that have frowned on all forms of gaming. This is true even when some measure of self-sorting and self-selecting procedures among the population in an area is assumed, as in Nevada, which is likely to attract people who have a predisposition toward gaming. Moreover, analysis of age-corrected data, which takes into account the comparative youthfulness of people in Nevada, still does not resolve the case favorably toward a lessening of illegal gaming in the face of state acceptance. What little analysis has been undertaken seems to confirm the belief that legal gaming begets a taste for action and an awareness of the supposed potential of broader schemes of chance. Rather than a corrective, it is a stimulus to widening participation in illegal games of chance.[23]

A deep sense of frustration sets in when the realities of laws against gambling are reviewed in terms of their effectiveness. It is two generations since Ernest Hemingway defined a Latin American republic as a place where the trains do not run on time, the mail does not get delivered, and lottery tickets are sold on the streets. One by one these characteristics have become part of the American scene. There has been a steady erosion of the moral posture of government, occasioned by widespread state-sponsored gambling. The argument has been made that the legalization of casino gaming is merely an extension of steps already taken in the cause of pari-mutuels, lotteries, jai-alai, and other betting games. While none of these events has shown any indication of reducing illegal gaming, the casinos, it is averred, are at least the penultimate action.

Legalization as a weapon against illegal gaming and its attendant corruptions is at best an overstated virtue. At worst it provides an environment that fosters criminal growth.

The Reality of Our Time?

There is a long and checkered – but not ignoble – tradition in the United States of regulating utilities. Essentially the latter are instrumentalities that are provided with monopoly status for the public good. The tempering factor, adjudicating between the needs of the corporate entity and the public it serves, typically is embodied in a whole matrix of statutory and administrative codes. These, in turn, are under the aegis of a regulatory commission whose members are appointed with greater or lesser attention to their experience and capacity. This is to do less than justice to a very complicated area – but the basic parameters are clear. In essence, the state of New Jersey granted a near monopoly to a place; casino gaming was to be permitted exclusively in Atlantic City.

In the course of the debates, and certainly embodied within the enabling legislation, was a series of goal statements, and indeed these incentives were needed to overcome the negative image that casino gaming was already imbued with. Provision was made for a Casino Control Commission to ensure appropriate operation of the casinos, commensurate with the public objectives. Is the failure to obtain those objectives a matter of structure? Or is there a dynamic of such intensity and dominance at work that willy-nilly would overcome the most rigorous of straitjackets?

In appraising the potential political influence of the casinos on public officials, it is essential to maintain perspective. A recent study by Common Cause, for example, based on reports filed by the Federal Election Commission, indicates that $6.5 million was given by political-action committees to top leaders of Congress in the 1980 election campaign, with almost two-thirds coming from business interests. Senator Robert Dole, the Republican chairman of the Senate Finance Committee, received $328,000 from political-action committees for his reelection campaign, with more than three-quarters of it, over $250,000, coming from business groups.[24]

The New Jersey regulatory structures specifically prohibit casinos from making political contributions. For the casinos to fly in the face of these injunctions would be to endanger their licenses. The case can be made that they are less politically active than other enterprises of the same scale that have a similar dependence on governmental goodwill.

Gerald Lynch, president of the John Jay College of Criminal Justice and chairman of the New York State Casino Gambling Panel, has espoused the view that the casinos are merely one among a large group of players in the political pigpen. Referring to the issue of whether the casinos would "pollute the political process," he commented that "with all the major corporations, the major industries, and lobbying groups in an election year, I don't see how the casino interests would come in and sweep the town of all these other vested interests."[25] The problem with this analysis is that the casinos, unlike an electric utility, do not have an organized counterweight. Anticasino forces rally briefly to bar them entry, then dissolve.

The casinos' sheer scale permits others, eager to curry their friendship or trade, to serve as their spokesmen. Robert R. Ferguson, chairman of First National State Bank, has continuously emphasized the danger that overregulation and high costs may hamper the prospects for the casinos' long-term success: "There is a growing and legitimate concern today among business people in New Jersey that the manner in which our state is carrying out its regulatory functions with respect to casino gaming – goes beyond what is necessary. They never were satisfied that it was necessary to license everything and everybody that moves in a casino hotel." The prospect of millions of dollars in revenues as well as jobs should prompt cooperation on the part of the state: "I believe that the enthusiasm and spirit of support which is essential will have to start with our state government. It is the obligation of the state government to do what it reasonably can to ensure a productive, healthy, and competitive climate in which casinos can do business."[26] Ferguson's institution, it should be noted, has engaged in substantial banking services for the casinos.

Similarly, when stock-market analysts suggest that the future of the casinos, and with them jobs and economic revitalization, are threatened by state "interference," legislators may listen. When Steven Eisenberg, an analyst at Bear-Stearns and Company, suggested that New Jersey must relax more gambling regulations before profit margins will improve significantly and casino developers will be willing to make new investments, major newspapers featured his comments.[27]

The jobs that the casinos create become hostages to the casinos' present and prospective goodwill. The casinos may not seem to be seeking a change from the present limited-hour rule in

Atlantic City, but quite unexpectedly their workers formed a committee for twenty-four hour gaming. The 30,000 persons with jobs directly dependent on the casinos represent a potent political reality.

The theory of countervailing forces assumes some invisible hand that tempers, if not the rapaciousness of individual claimants, then their overall success. The viability of this concept, when faced with the realities of the casinos' evasive power structures, as well as their unique requirements, is highly questionable. Whether the example is bureaucratic "creep," which has moved OTB and the lotteries from relatively passive absorbers of previous illegal wagering to very active advocates of their own growth, or the erosion of many of the limitations and safeguards first put into place in Atlantic City and since removed, the case is clear: gaming is more of a tiger than a housecat. Whereas the formalities of casino governance are ever more complex and expensive (over $30 million for fiscal 1982), there is still enough in the way of known credit swindles and skimming to raise questions as to whether any web of state security can be tight enough.[28]

The current generation of casino operators is experienced in walking in the shadow of criminals. The first large-scale hotel casino of Las Vegas started with gangster Bugsy Siegel, and links to criminals did not terminate with his abrupt demise. The offshore development of casinos in a variety of banana republics depended on close ties with whoever was in power, involving payoffs and using people competent to deal in this realm. The history of Resorts International, for example, is well documented on this score.[29]

There are also numerous ties between those with political influence and the casinos. Martin Greenberg, the former law partner of Governor Byrne of New Jersey (as well as a once-powerful state senator), joined the Golden Nugget as a top official: this may be an innocent association, but it is far from unique.[30] The *New York Times* post-Abscam editorial must be accepted as a fair summary: "The Abscam scandal in New Jersey, after only two years of casino activity, shows that gambling as a business is so rich, so fast, so powerful, and, perhaps inevitably, so unsavory that it cannot help but undermine government."[31]

Regulation creates a hunger for evasion and a temper for limiting or corrupting the regulators. The detailed way in which casinos are regulated and the risks and rewards built into the association of government and gaming provide a unique ground for corruption. Little organized opposition stands in the way of partnerships that wander far from the public interest. And casinos are particularly vulnerable to blackmail, whether from unions or regulators, because of their level of fixed costs and their sensitivity to licensing problems.

Could casinos ever become respectable? Is there some possibility that what we are dealing with are limitations of organizers and entrepreneurs who come from an unsavory age and bear with them the habits required by past illegitimacy? The rise of institutional banking relationships and funding sources has a potential for altering the crime and corruption-ridden antecedents of the casinos. Access to the Teamsters' Pension Fund is no longer the sole key to development. But habits are hard to break, and the issue of corruption cannot be casually disregarded.

It is nonsense to argue that if a state takes the first step, as it does when it approves off-track betting or a lottery, there can be no turning back. Before taking the next step, though, a state must examine all the costs and weigh them against the benefits, or presumed benefits. In our view, the costs of New Jersey's style of casino gambling as a means of revitalization far outweigh its virtues. This may not inhibit other states from moving into the arena. But it is our hope that the New Jersey experience will serve to guide them.

Tables

Notes

Index

TABLES

Table 1. New Jersey lottery gross sales and state share (millions of dollars)

Year	Gross sales	State share
1971	$ 78	$ 33
1972	138	69
1973	113	57
1974	89	46
1975	77	36
1976	158	66
1977	194	78
1978	238	96
1979	297	122
1980	349	146
1981	417	176

Source: New Jersey Lottery Commission, Trenton.

Table 2. Sources of contributions in support of casino gambling, 1976 referendum

Contributors listing Atlantic City address	$694,011	57%
Out-of-state contributors	261,297	22
Contributors listing New Jersey address other than Atlantic City	256,781	21

Contributors of $5,000 or more[a]	1976	1974[b]	Total, 1974 and 1976
Resorts International, N. Miami	$201,630	–	$201,630
Chalfonte-Haddon Hall[c], Atlantic City	52,235	12,000	64,235
The Press & Sunday Press, Atlantic City	45,000	11,800	56,800
Howard Johnson, Atlantic city	25,793	8,000	33,793
P & F Union Local 121	20,000	–	20,000
Atlantic City Holiday Inn, Atlantic City	17,450	20,000	27,450
Allegheny Airlines; Washington, D.C.	15,000	–	15,000
Atlantic City Assoc. Inc., Charleston, S.C.	14,000	–	14,000
Sheraton Deauville Hotel, Atlantic City	12,230	15,900	28,130
Atlantic City Convention Hall, Atlantic City	11,500	–	11,500
Marlboro-Blenheim, Atlantic City	11,000	6,000	17,000
Maxwell, R.C. Co., Trenton, Atlantic City	9,200	2,500	11,700
Kay Electric Co., Atlantic City	9,000	2,650	11,650
Ramada Inn Operating Co., Pleasantville	8,580	6,000	14,580
Taylor Supply Co., Pleasantville	6,400	650	7,050
Consolidated Laundries, New York	6,000	150	6,150
Atlantic City Airlines, Atlantic City	5,709	2,500	8,209
Cynwyd Investments, Bala Cynwyd, Pa.	5,500	–	5,500
Seashore Supply Co., Atlantic City	5,200	650	6,850
McGahn & Frias, Atlantic City	5,120	2,500	7,620
Arkboard Inc., Atlantic City	5,000	10,000	15,500
Atlantic Coast Liner, Atlantic City	5,000	–	5,000
Batzer, Steven, Mt. Laurel	5,000	–	5,000
Brigantine Castle, Brigantine	5,000	–	5,000
Colonial Frozen Foods, Atlantic City	5,000	2,500	7,500
Dillon, John, Ventnor	5,000	2,500	7,500
Ginsburg Bakery Superior Bakers, Inc., Atlantic City	5,000	–	5,000
Harrison Beverage Co., Pleasantville	5,000	2,500	7,500
Hertz Rent-A-Car System, Atlantic City	5,000	3,500	8,150
Polakoff, B. & Sons, Inc., Pleasantville	5,000	2,500	7,500
Rothenberg, Albert, Margate	5,000	2,500	7,500
7-Up Bottling Co. of Bridgeton	5,000	–	5,000
7-Up Bottling Co. of Camden, Gloucester	5,000	–	5,000
Total	$551,547	$106,950	$658,497

Table 2 (continued)

a. There were no contributors of more than $5,000 to the committees opposing the casino-gambling referendum.

b. The figures in the middle column represent contributions in support of the 1974 casino question.

c. Chalfonte-Haddon Hall is owned by Leeds & Lippincott Company, a fully owned subsidiary of Resorts International.

Table 3. Casino implementation chronology

1977

June 2	Casino Control Act signed
July 11	Joseph Lordi nominated to head commission
October 4	First Casino Control Commission meeting
December 22	Resorts International applies for license

1978

February 24	Bally's applies for license
March 17	Casino Control Act amended to permit temporary licenses
May 28	Resorts International opens
September 1	Caesars Boardwalk Regency applies for license
November 8	Resorts temporary license extended three months

1979

February 2	Resorts temporary license
May	CCC requires a full hotel renovation
July	Caesars opens
September 18	Governor signs tax-rate increases
December	Bally's opens

1980

February 2	Abscam investigation announced
February 4	Commissioner MacDonald resigns
May 20	Governor signs CCC reconstitution bill

Table 4. Regulatory changes affecting Atlantic City casino hotels

Regulation	Potential impact	Status
Enacted		
Minimum-maximum: allowable bets (all table games): $2 minimum discarded favor of $5 minimum	Improves table drop and hold percentage	Formally effective Feb. 4, 1981
Early surrender (blackjack)	Improves table drop and hold percentage	Effective July 15, 1981 (emergency basis), formally effective Oct. 8, 1981
"En prison" (roulette)	Improves table drop and hold percentage	Formally effective Sept. 25, 1981
Nightly live entertainment	Now at discretion of management	Formally effective Oct. 5, 1981
Advertising	Pre-notification to commission of copy no longer required	Formally effective Oct. 8, 1981
Additional cards (blackjack)	Dealer no longer must draw additional cards if all decisions for or against players have been reached; increases velocity of play	Formally effective June 15, 1981
Slot change personnel	No minimum requirement necessary (reduction in payroll/expenses)	Formally effective Feb. 1, 1981
Security personnel	Reduction in payroll/expenses	CCC allowed operators to staff on a case-by-case basis with approval of CCC
Proposed		
Supervisory personnel (craps)	Modification of requirement that an additional boxman be available in pit area (reduction in payroll/ expenses	Available for adoption
Licensing of hotel-related employees	From license to simple registration – reduction in license fees and less pirating of previously licensed personnel	Legislature to review
24-hour gaming at discretion of management	Increase drop/win; labor expense also increases	Legislature to review
Junket pre-notification	5-day, instead of 15-day, $200 threshold to be raised to higher level before casinos must notify CCC of players' names	CCC to review early 1982

Source; *Gaming Business Magazine,* April 1982, p. 16.

Table 5. Employment shifts, 1960-1975

	1960	1965	Change, 1960-1965 Number	Percent
New Jersey	1,581,128	1,753,845	172,717	10.9%
Atlantic County	40,403	45,484	5,081	12.6
Atlantic City	24,821	26,569	1,748	7.0
Essex County	305,903	315,911	10,008	3.3
Newark City	200,972	201,871	899	0.4
Hudson County	195,837	198,186	2,349	1.2
Jersey City	66,731	66,234	− 497	− 0.7
Camden County	90,812	96,120	5,308	5.8
City of Camden	58,883	49,121	− 9,762	− 16.6

	1965	1970	Change, 1965-1970 Number	Percent
New Jersey	1,753,845	2,095,798	341,953	19.7%
Atlantic County	45,484	51,581	6,097	13.4
Atlantic City	26,569	25,069	− 1,500	− 5.6
Essex County	315,911	326,151	10,240	3.2
Newark City	201,871	186,602	− 15,269	− 7.6
Hudson County	198,186	213,169	14,983	7.6
Jersey City	66,234	71,600	5,366	8.1
Camden County	96,120	115,256	19,136	19.9
City of Camden	49,121	41,584	− 7,537	− 15.3

	1970	1975	Change, 1970-1975 Number	Percent
New Jersey	2,095,798	2,217,132	121,334	5.8%
Atlantic County	51,581	51,803	222	0.4
Atlantic City	25,069	22,039	− 3,030	− 12.1
Essex County	326,151	304,515	− 21,636	− 6.6
Newark City	186,602	145,659	− 40,943	− 21.9
Hudson County	213,169	182,694	− 30,475	− 14.2
Jersey City	71,600	59,506	− 12,094	− 16.9
Camden County	115,256	123,578	8,322	7.2
City of Camden	41,584	33,307	− 8,277	− 19.9

Note: Data are for September of the respective years.
Source: New Jersey, Department of Labor and Industry, Division of Planning and Research, *Covered Employment Trends in New Jersey*, monthly.

Table 6. Atlantic City employment by sector, 1960-1975

Sector	1960	1965	Change, 1960-1965		1970	Change, 1965-1970		1975	Change, 1970-1975	
			Number	Percent		Number	Percent		Number	Percent
Manufacturing	2,226	2,636	410	18.4%	1,923	−713	−27.0%	1,810	−113	−5.9%
Wholesale and retail trade	8,586	9,644	1,058	12.3	9,621	−23	−0.2	7,567	−2,054	−21.3
Transportation	813	718	−95	−11.7	467	−251	−35.0	366	−101	−21.6
Communications and public utilities	1,605	1,398	−207	−12.9	1,663	265	19.0	709	−954	−57.3
Services	9,017	9,472	455	5.0	9,202	−270	−2.9	9,453	251	2.7
Finance, insurance, and real estate	1,518	1,622	104	6.9	1,200	−422	−26.0	1,464	264	21.8
Contract construction	1,011	1,049	38	3.8	965	−84	−8.0	639	−325	−33.8
Mining, agriculture and other	45	30	−15	−33.3	28	−2	−6.6	31	3	10.7
Total	24,821	26,569	1,748	7.0	25,069	−1,500	−5.6	22,039	−3,030	−12.1

Note: Data are September of the respective years.
Source: New Jersey, Department of Labor and Industry, Division of Planning and Research, *Covered Employment Trends in New Jersey*, monthly.

Table 7. Employment shifts, 1975-1980

	Total employment			
			Change, 1975-1980	
	1975	1980	Number	Percent
New Jersey	2,217,132	2,528,845	311,713	14.1%
Atlantic County	51,803	76,884	25,081	48.4
Atlantic City	22,039	36,388	14,349	65.1
Essex County	304,515	308,155	3,640	1.2
Newark City	145,659	130,552	− 15,107	− 10.4
Hudson County	182,694	180,224	− 2,470	− 1.4
Jersey City	59,506	57,756	− 1,750	− 2.9
Camden County	123,578	139,299	15,721	12.7
City of Camden	33,307	27,926	− 5,345	− 16.0

	Atlantic City			
			Change, 1975-1980	
Sector	1975	1980	Number	Percent
Manufacturing	1,810	1,031	− 779	− 43.0%
Wholesale and				
retail trade	7,567	6,496	− 1,071	− 14.2
Wholesale	862	692	− 170	− 19.7
Retail	6,705	5,804	− 901	− 13.4
Transportation	366	606	240	65.6
Communications				
and public utilities	709	832	123	17.3
Services	9,453	24,225	14,771	156.3
Finance, insurance,				
and real estate	1,464	1,274	− 190	− 13.0
Contract construc-				
tion	639	1,919	1,280	200.3
Mining, agriculture				
and other	31	6	− 25	− 80.6
Total	22,039	36,388	14,349	65.1

Note: Data are for September of the respective years.

Source: New Jersey, Department of Labor and Industry, Division of Planning and Research, *Covered Employment Trends in New Jersey,* monthly.

Table 8. Employment shifts, 1980–1981

| | Total employment | | | |
| | 1980 | 1981 | Change, 1980–1981 | |
			Number	Percent
New Jersey	2,528,845	2,589,641	160,796	2.4%
Atlantic County	76,884	87,270	10,386	13.5
Atlantic City	36,388	42,859	6,471	17.8
Essex County	308,155	303,754	− 4,401	− 1.4
Newark City	130,552	126,850	− 3,702	− 2.8
Hudson County	180,224	178,187	− 2,037	− 1.1
Jersey City	57,756	55,903	− 1,853	− 3.2
Camden County	139,299	141,927	2,628	1.9
City of Camden	27,926	27,643	− 283	− 1.0

| | Atlantic City | | | |
| | | | Change, 1980–1981 | |
Sector	1980	1981	Number	Percent
Manufacturing	1,031	1,002	− 29	− 2.8%
Wholesale and				
retail trade	6,496	6,316	− 180	− 2.8
Wholesale	692	677	− 15	− 2.2
Retail	5,804	5,639	− 165	− 2.8
Transportation	606	579	− 27	− 4.5
Communications				
and public utilities	832	848	16	1.9
Services	24,225	31,669	7,444	30.7
Finance, insurance,				
and real estate	1,274	1,097	− 177	− 13.9
Contract construc-				
tion	1,919	1,343	− 576	− 30.0
Mining, agriculture				
and other	6	5	− 1	− 16.7
Total	36,388	42,859	6,471	17.8

Note: Data are for September of the respective years.

Source: New Jersey, Department of Labor and Industry, Division of Planning and Research, *Covered Employment Trends in New Jersey,* monthly.

Table 9. Atlantic City employment by sector

Sector	1970	1975	1976	1977	1978	1979	1980	1981
Manufacturing	1,923	1,810	1,518	1,452	1,063	1,045	1,031	1,002
Wholesale trade	9,621	862	888	952	885	785	692	677
Retail trade		6,705	6,869	6,502	6,983	6,238	5,804	5,639
Transportation	467	366	352	306	489	513	606	579
Communications and public utilities	1,663	709	704	715	776	835	832	848
Services	9,202	9,453	10,292	9,488	11,640	17,992	24,224	31,669
Finance, insurance, and real estate	1,200	1,464	1,307	1,155	1,292	1,343	1,274	1,097
Contract construction	965	639	656	868	907	2,726	1,919	1,343
Mining, agriculture and other	28	31	15	15	11	12	6	5
Total	25,069	22,039	22,601	21,453	24,046	31,489	36,388	42,859

Note: Data are for September of the respective years.

Source: New Jersey, Department of Labor and Industry, Division of Planning and Research, *Covered Employment Trends in New Jersey*, monthly.

Table 10. Shifting industrial structures, 1970–1980

Sector	New Jersey			Atlantic County			Atlantic City		
	1970	1975	1980	1970	1975	1980	1970	1975	1980
Manufacturing	41.4%	34.3%	31.1%	19.0%	16.9%	11.5%	7.7%	8.2%	2.8%
Wholesale and Retail trade	25.7	27.4	27.1	35.8	35.5	41.8	38.4	34.3	17.9
Transportation	5.2	4.7	4.3	2.0	1.9	1.8	1.9	1.7	1.7
Communications and public utilities	3.2	2.9	3.2	5.1	4.3	3.4	6.6	3.2	2.3
Services	12.7	19.0	22.6	25.1	28.1	26.3	36.7	42.9	66.6
Finance, insurance, and real estate	4.8	6.1	6.2	5.8	7.7	6.1	4.8	6.6	3.5
Contract construction	6.0	4.9	4.6	6.7	5.0	6.4	3.8	2.9	5.3
Mining, agriculture, and other	1.0	0.8	0.9[a]	0.5	0.5	2.8[a]	0.1	0.1	0.0

a. Definitional change.

Source: New Jersey, Department of Labor and Industry, Division of Planning and Research, *Covered Employment Trends in New Jersey*, monthly.

Table 11. A typical casino's employment

Income category	Total		Share of income category	
	Number	Percent	Female	Minority
$50,000 and over	32	0.8%	6%	13%
$40,000-49,999	59	1.5	14	5
$35,000-39,999	310	7.9	35	12
$30,000-34,999	122	3.1	25	16
$25,000-29,999	33	0.8	15	18
$20,000-24,999	162	4.1	20	15
$15,000-19,999	395	10.0	37	34
$10,000-14,999	1,526	38.7	58	43
$ 5,000- 9,999	1,300	33.0	46	23
Total	3,939	100.0	-	-

Table 12. Unemployment parameters (numbers in thousands)

Year	Civilian labor force	Resident employment	Unemployment	Unemployment rate
Atlantic City				
1979	95.2	86.3	8.8	9.4%
1980	103.9	95.2	8.6	8.3
1981	114.7	105.1	9.6	8.4
New Jersey				
1979	3,538	3,293	245	6.9%
1980	3,582	3,324	258	7.2
1981	3,578	3,316	262	7.3

Source: New Jersey, Department of Labor and Industry, Division of Planning and Research

Table 13. Atlantic City assessments of casinos

Casino	1977	1980	1982
Resorts	$8,326,600	$56,595,900	$89,123,300
Caesars	5,864,000	45,744,200	72,968,000
Bally's	3,444,100	75,954,660	114,180,460
The Sands	1,817,400	54,504,700	54,504,700
Harrah's	215,300	8,564,750	109,230,800
Golden Nugget	1,810,700	9,000,400	96,774,400
Playboy-Elsinore	1,306,200	3,386,400	91,807,500
Claridge	2,237,900	4,058,700	69,909,000
Ramada's Tropicana	1,688,300	8,291,200	133,073,700
Total casino assessment	26,710,500	266,100,860	831,571,860
Total assessment base (total assessed valuation of city)	308,877,020	863,844,921	1,528,128,057
Casino share of total assessments	8.6%	30.8%	54.4%

Source: Atlantic City Casino Hotel Association; Atlantic City Property Assessment Office.

Table 14. Assessed and market valuations in Atlantic City (millions of dollars)

Year	Total assessed valuation	Market equalized valuation	Equalization ratio
1972	$334.0	$353.2	.9914
1973	328.0	346.8	.9999
1974	321.9	357.5	.9567
1975	318.7	383.8	.8734
1976	316.6	381.0	.8740
1977	308.9	364.0	.8894
1978	306.4	447.7	.7133
1979	665.1	552.8	1.2834
1980	863.8	1,279.8	.6909
1981	1,210.1	1,976.1	.6246
1982	1,528.1	3,238.6	.4776

Note: Market valuation is the total on which county taxes are apportioned.
Source: Atlantic County Board of Taxation, *Abstract of Ratables* (Atlantic City, annual).

Table 15. Assessed and equalized tax rates in Atlantic City

Year	Total assessed tax rate	Total equalized tax rate	Component assessed tax rates		
			Education	Municipal	County
1972	5.11	4.84	1.52	2.72	.87
1973	5.27	4.98	1.67	2.73	.87
1974	6.50	5.86	1.51	4.09	.89
1975	6.65	5.53	1.45	4.19	1.01
1976	7.87	6.54	1.46	5.35	1.06
1977	7.95	6.75	1.45	5.51	.98
1978	7.14	4.87	1.48	4.46	1.20
1979	3.62	4.35	.79	2.28	.54
1980	4.07	2.75	.99	2.25	.83
1981	5.04	3.10	.98	3.29	.77
1982	4.50	2.14	.90	2.70	.89

Note: Rates expressed per $100 valuation (assessed or equalized).

Source: Atlantic County Board of Taxation, *Abstract of Ratables* (Atlantic City, annual); New Jersey Department of the Treasury, Division of Taxation, annual reports (Trenton).

Table 16. Atlantic City property-tax levies (millions of dollars)

Year	Total property tax levy	Sector		
		Education	Municipal	County
1972	$17.1	$ 5.1	$ 9.1	$ 2.9
1973	17.3	5.5	9.0	2.9
1974	20.9	4.9	13.2	2.9
1975	21.2	4.6	13.4	3.2
1976	24.9	4.6	16.9	3.3
1977	24.6	4.5	17.0	3.0
1978	21.8	4.5	13.7	3.7
1979	24.1	5.3	15.2	3.6
1980	35.1	8.5	19.5	7.1
1981	61.0	11.8	39.8	9.3
1982	68.7	13.8	41.3	13.7

Source: Atlantic County Board of Taxation, *Abstract of Ratables* (Atlantic City, annual); New Jersey Department of the Treasury, Division of Taxation, annual reports (Trenton).

Table 17. Assessed valuation of real property in Atlantic City

Property	1977		1980	
	Amount	Percent	Amount	Percent
Vacant	$11,683,355	4.02%	$149,577,680	17.64%
Residential	80,699,965	27.80	126,412,235	14.91
Commercial	168,967,040	58.21	519,808,235	61.31
Industrial	1,262,900	.44	2,992,100	.35
Apartments	27,674,250	9.53	49,054,650	5.79
Total	290,287,510	100	847,844,900	100

Note: Data encompass only real-property assessments, not total valuation.

Source: New Jersey Department of Community Affairs, Division of Local Government Services, annual reports (Trenton).

TABLES

Table 18. Luxury-tax receipts in Atlantic City

1970	$3,714,150
1971	3,293,273
1972	3,149,009
1973	3,006,909
1974	3,125,570
1975	2,842,119
1976	2,868,260
1977	2,888,631
1978	3,668,222
1979	4,571,840
1980[a]	5,791,000
1981[a]	7,784,100

a. Atlantic City's share was reduced to 4 percent in fiscal year 1980 and 3 percent in 1981. The city secured $4.9 million in 1980 and $4.6 million in 1981. Prior to 1980, all receipts accrued to Atlantic City.

Source: New Jersey Department of Community Affairs, Division of Local Government Service, annual reports (Trenton).

Table 19. Casino revenues and tax summary, 1978–1982

Year	Total gross revenues[a]	Number of days in operation	Daily average gross revenue	Adjustment for uncollectables	Gross revenues after adjustment	Tax[b]
1978	$ 134,073,445	220	$ 609,425	$ 400,000	$ 133,673,445	$10,693,876
1979	325,480,531	365	891,727	1,010,908	324,469,623	34,390,725
1980	642,673,245	366	1,755,638	19,135,671	623,537,574	68,635,460[c]
1981	1,099,782,762	365	3,013,103	18,465,738	1,081,317,024	86,505,361
1982	1,493,164,081	365	4,090,860	25,439,246	1,467,724,835	117,440,439[d]
Total	3,695,174,064	1,681	2,198,200	64,451,563	3,630,722,501	317,665,861

a. Gross casino revenue or "win" represents what the casino wins from the patrons before taxes and expenses are deducted.

b. Assembly Bill No. 3602, signed on September 18, 1979, calls for an effective tax rate of 12 percent when two or three licensed casinos are in operation, 10 percent when four licensed casinos are in operation (August 1980), and 8 percent when five or more licensed casinos are in operation (November 1980).

c. Includes a $319,392 penalty imposed by the Casino Control Commission and paid by Resorts.

d. Includes $19,653 in delinquent taxes and $2,800 in interest paid by Sands. Does not include $1,981,110 interest earned from April through November 1982. (December 1982 interest total not available.)

Source: New Jersey Casino Control Commission, *Annual Report, 1981* (Trenton); New Jersey Casino Control Commission, monthly reports, January–December 1982 (Trenton).

Table 20. Caesars Boardwalk Regency, tax disbursements, August 1, 1979–July 31, 1980 (unaudited)

Federal taxes			
Corporate income tax		$13,992,000	
Slot machine tax		90,300	
Payroll taxes			
Social security	$3,533,000		
Federal unemployment	242,000	3,775,000	
Total federal taxes			$17,857,300
New Jersey state taxes			
Corporate income tax		3,426,000	
New Jersey sales and use tax		105,000	
Food sales tax		554,000	
Payroll taxes			
NJ disability and NJ unemployment		1,628,000	
Casino-related state taxes			
Slot-machine tax	732,400		
Casino gross revenue tax	23,403,000	24,135,400	
Total New Jersey state taxes			$29,848,400
Atlantic City taxes			
Luxury tax			
Room revenues	443,000		
Beverage sales	242,000		
Showroom tickets	112,000		
Special events	15,000	812,000	
Property taxes		1,834,000	
Total Atlantic City taxes			$2,646,000
Total taxes paid			$50,351,700

Source: Caesars Boardwalk Regency.

Table 21. Median sales prices of residential structures sold, Atlantic City municipalities (one to three units in structure)

				Percent change	
Municipality	1972	1976	1980	1972-1976	1976-1980
Absecon	$21,400	$30,500	$62,500	42.5%	104.9%
Atlantic City	13,500	15,000	37,000	11.1	146.7
Brigantine	22,500	34,000	72,950	51.1	114.6
Buena	18,950	21,000	30,000	10.8	42.9
Buena Vista	14,500	24,900	31,950	71.1	28.3
Corbin[a]	15,000	20,500	30,000	-	-
Egg Harbor City	15,225	20,000	32,800	31.4	64.0
Egg Harbor Twp.	16,500	25,500	48,000	54.5	88.2
Estell Manor[a]	5,900	11,125	41,000	-	-
Folsom[a]	13,000	27,200	37,000	-	-
Galloway	14,900	25,750	48,000	72.8	86.4
Hamilton	14,000	23,900	50,000	70.7	109.2
Hammonton	21,000	26,000	32,200	23.8	23.8
Linwood	22.500	29,000	68,200	28.9	135.2
Longport	35,000	42,500	110,000	21.4	158.8
Margate	29,375	39,000	111,250	32.8	185.3
Mullica	12,000	22,500	33,450	87.5	48.7
Northfield	22,000	30,450	62,100	38.4	103.9
Pleasantville	12,000	16,000	29,500	33.3	84.4
Port Republic[a]	16,000	25,200	68,000	-	-
Somers Point	20,700	29,000	57,500	40.1	98.3
Ventnor	25,250	33,800	80,000	33.9	136.7
Weymouth[a]	9,000	32,900	37,375	-	-

a. Number of sales insufficient for statistical significance.
Source: New Jersey Division of Taxation data, tabulated by CUPR.

Table 22. Crime index for Atlantic City, Atlantic County, and New Jersey

| | Atlantic City | | | New Jersey | | |
| | | Change from previous year | | | Change from previous year | |
Year	Crime index	Number	Percent	Crime index	Number	Percent
1981	12,594	695	5.8	457,405	− 12,764	− 2.7
1980	11,899	4,889	69.7	470,169	44,279	10.4
1979	7,010	1,272	22.2	425,890	44,350	11.6
1978	5,738	1,347	30.7	381,540	6,680	1.8
1977	4,391	− 298	− 6.4	374,860	− 21,680	− 5.5
1976	4,689	− 165	− 3.4	396,540	20,401	5.4
1975	4,854	227	4.9	376,139	26,005	7.4
1974	4,627	− 229	− 4.7	350,134	49,958	16.6
1973	4,856	− 315	− 6.1	300,176	17,145	6.1
1972	5,171	− 1,213	− 19.0	283,031	− 6,505	− 2.2
1971	6,384	− 365	− 5.4	289,536	33,358	13.0
1970	6,749	-	-	256,178	-	-

Note: Crime index: the sum total of seven major offenses used to measure the extent, fluctuation, and distribution of crime in a geographical area. The following crimes make up the index: murder, forcible rape, robbery, aggravated assault, burglary, larceny-theft, and motor vehicle theft. These offenses are referred to as Index offenses.

Source: *Uniform Crime Reports: State of New Jersey*, annual reports, 1970-1981, New Jersey State Police, Trenton; *New Jersey Uniform Crime Report, 1981*, preliminary annual release, New Jersey State Police, Trenton; Bureau of Crime Analysis, Atlantic City Police Department, Atlantic City.

Table 23. Detailed crime increases, Atlantic City

Crime	1977	1978	1979	1980	1981
Pickpocket	15	131	231	544	1,247
Pursesnatch	156	129	229	403	231
Shoplifting	66	74	185	269	292
Larceny from motor vehicles	400	639	914	1,897	1,788
Larceny, MV parts/accessories	285	329	408	590	580
Larceny of bikes	210	190	246	269	174
Larceny from buildings	826	854	1,312	3,660	4,378
Larceny from coin machines	2	8	19	33	45
Larceny, all others	161	191	244	368	327
Stolen auto	469	605	874	1,216	1,067
Index crimes					
Homicide	10	12	9	11	17
Rape	27	36	63	51	63
Robbery	257	339	432	644	783
Assaults	579	685	1,528	1,616	1,723
Breaking and entering	1,457	1,742	1,495	1,620	1,223
Total	4,920	5,964	8,189	13,191	13,938

Source: *Uniform Crime Reports: State of New Jersey*, annual reports, 1970-1981, New Jersey State Police, Trenton; Bureau of Crime Analysis Atlantic City Police Department.

Table 24. Total casino revenue (win) by selected game type, Atlantic City, July 1981

Game	Amount	Percent
Table games	63,749,711	54.0%
Blackjack	30,831,473	26.1
Craps	20,649,775	17.5
Other	12,268,463	10.4
Coin-operated Devices	54,280,227	46.0
5¢ and 25¢ slot machines	35,151,925	29.8
$1 slot machines and other	19,128,302	16.2
Total	118,029,938	100.0

Source: New Jersey Casino Control Commission, monthly report.

NOTES

1. The Semimagic Bullet

1. Dean Witter Reynolds, *Gaming Abstract*, April 1979. This leading Wall Street firm has become a font of information on the casinos.

2. Consad Research Corporation, *The Development of Regional Automobile Location Evaluation System* (Washington, D.C., 1981, processed).

3. U.S. Bureau of the Census, *Statistical Abstract of the United States* (Washington, D.C.: U.S. Government Printing Office, 1980), p. 307.

4. In the gambling industry the term "win" refers to the house's take, not to the patron's winnings. It is the difference between the total gambled and the returns given the patron.

5. Commission on the Review of the National Policy Toward Gambling (CRNPTG), *Gambling in America, Final Report* (Washington, D.C.: U.S. Government Printing Office, 1976), table 3.7 on pp. 41-42. This multivolume report is possibly the most substantial effort by the federal government to outline the parameters of gambling.

6. Ibid., p. 49.

7. Ibid., p. 85.

8. *Gallup Opinion Index*, Report No. 161, p. 6-13.

9. Dean Witter Reynolds, *Lodging Industry Periodical*, 1980, p. 4.

10. Ibid.

11. Laventhol and Horwath, *First Annual Gaming Conference – Gaming Industry*, New York, October 1979, p. 6. The sponsor of this report is the premier accounting firm in the hospitality and gaming industry.

13. Laventhol and Horwath, *Second Annual Gaming Conference*, New York, October 1980, p. 21.

14. Interview with Albert J. Merck, January 26, 1981.

15. Las Vegas Convention Visitors Authority, *Las Vegas Visitor Profile Study – 1976-77*, Las Vegas, n.d. [1977].

16. CRNPTG, *Gambling in America*, pp. 96, 97.

17. William R. Eadington, *The Economics of Gambling Behavior: A Qualitative Study of Nevada's Gambling Industry* (Bureau of Business and Economic Research, University of Nevada, Reno, 1973).

18. See Chapter 6.

19. *Wall Street Journal*, November 5, 1980, p. 29.

20. Confidential interview, January 29, 1981.

2. The State and Gambling

1. For general histories of gambling in the United States, see Henry Chafetz, *Play the Devil: A History of Gambling in the United States from 1492 to 1955* (New York: Clarkson N. Potter, 1960), and Stephen Longstreet, *Win or Lose: A Social History of Gambling in America* (New York: Bobbs-Merril, 1977). The report of the CRNPTG, *Gambling in America*, submitted to Congress and the President in 1976, contains a brief history of various types of gambling. On lotteries see Chafetz, pp. 20-27.

2. Chafetz, pp. 397, 398.

3. Ibid.

4. Ibid., pp. 299-308.

5. Ibid.

6. CRNPTG, *Gambling in America*, pp. 146, 147. See pp. 11-25 of this report for a summary of federal gambling statutes.

7. For an excellent history and analysis of the New Hampshire lottery, see "The Economics of State-Operated Lotteries" by Sam Rosen, in CRNPTG, *Gambling in America*, appendix 1, pp. 805-815.

8. On reasons for the failure of the New Hampshire lottery to meet expectations, see Rosen, p. 808, and CRNPTG, *Gambling in America*, p. 146. On federal statutes, see CRNPTG, *Gambling in America*, pp. 18, 19, 145, 146.

9. Rosen, p. 809.

10. This legislative review can be found in New Jersey, Senate Judiciary Committee, *Public Hearing on Senate Concurrent Resolution*, No. 7, June 1, 1966, pp. 5-7.

11. Ibid. On the figures that lottery proponents used, see New Jersey, *Public Hearing before Gambling Study Commission*, December 6, 1974, p. 2A.

12. Gross receipts jumped in the New Jersey lottery after 1976. The reasons for the increase suggested by the commission are twofold: (1) the lottery

was allowed to advertise itself via the mass media after 1975; (2) inflation. More people were willing to spend less-valuable dollars   in hope of winning more.

13. CRNPTG, *Gambling in America*, p. 146. The Ritchie quote is in the Rosen article, p. 809.

14. Profits from the New Jersey lottery make up about 3 percent of the state's budget. The exact percentages are: 1978 – 2.5 percent; 1979 – 2.0 percent; 1980 – 3.2 percent; 1981 – 3.2 percent; 1982 – 2.9 percent (the last two figures are projections). These data were obtained in a telephone conversation with the Office of the Budget, Trenton, March 1981. In New York the lottery must pay 45 percent of its income to the state's education budget, of which it provides 2 percent. The lottery produces about $187 to $190 million out of a total state budget of approximately $15 to $16 billion. These figures were obtained in a telephone conversation with the New York State Lottery Commission, Albany, March 1981.

15. *New York Times*, January 12, 1969, p. 30. CRNPTG, *Gambling in America*, pp. 105-107, gives a brief history of the racing industry.

16. *New York Times*, February 13, 1969, p. 1; February 14, 1969, p. 38.

17. Ibid., March 5, 1969, p. 33.

18. Ibid., July 29, 1969, p. 24.

19. Ibid., September 7, 1969, p. 1; October 13, 1969, p. 50.

20. Ibid., March 4, 1970; April 18, 1970, p. 16; April 19, 1970, p. 68; April 21, 1970, p. 3; April 24, 1970, p. 31.

21. Ibid., February 27, 1969, p. 28.

22. Ibid., August 24, 1970, p. 1; August 30, 1970, p. 23; October 1, 1970, p. 10; December 18, 1970, p. 1.

23. Ibid., March 3, 1971, p. 1; April 17, 1971, p. 1; CRNPTG, *Gambling in America*, p. 134.

24. *New York Times*, May 19, 1973, p. 1

25. Ibid., January 10, 1974, p. 1. The issue of police corruption by gambling interests is not new; Lincoln Steffens documented it well in the early twentieth century. The issue is examined in depth by Allan K. Kornblum in his *The Moral Hazards: Police Strategies for Honesty and Ethical Behavior*. (Lexington, Mass.: D. C. Heath, 1976). No one knows the size, influence, or total revenue figures for organized-crime gambling operations. The CRNPTG report of 1976 discussed illegal gambling but skirted the question of a dollar figure. Rufus King reported that illegal gambling brought in over $7 billion annually – see his *Gambling and Organized Crime* (Washington, D. C.: Public Affairs Press, 1969), pp. 7-10. In 1974, the Twentieth Century Fund and the Fund for the City of New York issued a report on legalized gambling titled *Easy Money* which suggested that illegal gambling revenues were higher than many people suspected; yet the report was careful to acknowledge that estimates of this illegal income were only speculation.

26. *New York Times*, January 11, 1979, p. 1.

27. On March 5, 1981, Mayor Edward Koch announced that he would push to allow OTB offices to take bets on all sports. The resulting income would go toward shoring up the failing New York transit system. OTB receipts have risen since 1976. Much of this rise, however, went to operating expenses. The city and state shares remained almost constant and in 1982 sharply declined.

28. For descriptions of this period, see Chafetz, pp. 32-178, and Longstreet, pp. 42-113.

29. For a fascinating history of Saratoga, see Longstreet, pp. 57-88. Chafetz recounts this period on pp. 318-339.

30. The immediate circumstances of Parkhurst and his reform group's victory are told in Chafetz, pp. 340-349. A much more thorough and perceptive account can be found in *The Autobiography of Lincoln Steffens* (New York: Harcourt, Brace and World, 1931), pp. 197-291. *The Autobiography*, especially volume 2, vividly describes the initial hopes of reformers and their utter inability to halt crime, vice, and corruption, with a few notable exceptions. On the moral and political climate of the Progressive period, see George E. Mowry, *The Era of Theodore Roosevelt and the Birth of Modern America 1900-1912* (New York: Harper and Row, 1958), and Robert H. Wiebe, *The Search for Order, 1877-1920* (New York: Hill and Wang, 1967).

31. Wallace Turner, *Gambler's Money: The New Force in American Life* (Boston: Houghton Mifflin, 1965), p. 31.

32. For the traditional view, see King, pp. 23-26. A more thorough and documented history of the connection between bootlegging and gambling is in CRNPTG, *Gambling in America*, appendix 1, pp. 102-43.

33. Turner, pp. 31-62. Also see Fred J. Cook, *A Two-Dollar Bet Means Murder* (New York: Dial Press, 1961), pp. 172-202.

34. Turner, p. 39.

35. Ibid., pp. 39, 40.

36. There is a vivid description of this in Susan Berman's memoir of her father, long-time manager of the Flamingo, in *Easy Street* (New York: Dial Press, 1981). Gambling and gangsters clearly went hand in hand, but most of the outside world was oblivious of the linkage.

37. CRNPTG, *Gambling in America*, pp. 72-84.

38. Ibid., pp. 83-86.

39. *Rouge et Noir, Resort Management Report*, March 31, 1981, p. 2.

3. The Casino Passage

1. Statistics from Economics Research Associates, *Impact of Casino Gambling on the Redevelopment Potential of the Uptown Urban Renewal Site and on the Economy of Atlantic City* (Washington, D.C., June 1976).

2. *Newsweek*, June 8, 1970, p. 86

3. Common usage-see Greg Walker "The Only Game in Town,"

Philadelphia Magazine, August 1971, p. 91.

4. Neither political party was totally lacking in power (or corruption). A favorite practice of political boss Nucky Johnson and later of Farley was to reward helpful Democrats by keeping them at a certain level of power, thereby assuring that the opposition party was not in a position to adopt a high moral attitude and seek reform. *New York Times*, July 23, 1941, p. 35.

5. Charles Funnell, *By the Beautiful Sea: The Rise and High Times of That Great American Resort, Atlantic City* (New York: Knopf, 1975), pp. 93-98.

6. Al Johnson was removed from this position in December 1942. See *New York Times*, January 1, 1942, p. 17.

7. "For more than two decades he has had a wide reputation as a lavish entertainer at mass parties, picnics, and nightclubs both in Atlantic City and in New York." *New York Times*, May 11, 1939, p. 2

8. Jack Alexander, "That's How They Got Nucky Johnson," *Readers' Digest*, May 1942, p. 79.

9. Ibid., p. 80.

10. Ibid., p. 86.

11. Nucky Johnson was paroled on August 15, 1945, after serving four years of the ten-year sentence.

12. Walter, "The Only Game in Town," p. 53.

13. D. W. Naus, "Gambling on Reform," *New Jersey Reporter*, March 1980, p. 13.

14. Frank L. Smith, quoted under oath, in *Transcript of the Hearings before the Special Committee to Investigate Organized Crime in Interstate Commerce: United States Senate, 82nd Congress* (Washington, D.C., 1951, U.S. Y4, C86/2).

15. George McCallum, quoted under oath, in ibid.

16. *New York Times*, July 20, 1951, p. 11.

17. The four policemen, Francis B. Gribbin, John J. Mooney, Jack Portock, and Frederick Warlich, were cleared of the extortion charges brought against them and were reinstated on the Atlantic City police force on December 31, 1952. The city's charges were never very well defined, as the New Jersey State Civil Service Commission remarked at the time: "the applicants have sustained their appeal by the greater weight of evidence . . . and the action of the Authorities of Atlantic City is reversed and set aside." *New York Times*, January 1, 1953, p. 18.

18. A "Democratic leader," quoted in ibid., July 22, 1951, p. 56.

19. Vote count: 11,128 to 6,407: from *The Press*, November 8, 1953, p. 1. This is the leading Atlantic City newspaper.

20. Walter, "The Only Game in Town," p. 53.

21. An "Atlantic City civic leader," quoted in *New York Times*, June 9, 1965, p. 17.

22. Residents of Atlantic City were finally able to vote directly for a mayor for the first time in seventy years on May 12, 1982 – and a recall is likely in 1983!

23. Commissioner Pierre Hollingsworth, quoted in Naus, "Gambling on Reform," p. 13.

24. Frank Farley's long-time association with Orman was well documented during the hearings before the Kefauver committee held in Atlantic City in the summer of 1951. A veritable parade of witnesses, from bookies to bank presidents, all agreed that the relationship was definitely not on "the up-and-up." What they could not agree on was whether Farley ran Orman or vice versa. The only thing Farley would ever say about the matter, then or afterward, was that he once represented Orman as his attorney and that he "attends gatherings with Orman at one time or another." See *Transcript of the Hearings*, pp. 394-405, 38-32, 190-217.

25. Farley, quoted in *New York Times*, January 9, 1969, p. 23.

26. Patrick McGahn, quoted in ibid., February 5, 1969, p. 26.

27. Article by Ronald Sullivan in ibid., p. 26.

28. Farley's investment in the Atlantic City race track is often cited as one of his most obvious displays of greed. He got the track located in Atlantic County as a regional offset to the Monmouth track built at the same time. He then acted as attorney for the track and collected nearly $1 million in stock from it through the years. "I've got a right, just like anybody else, to make a little money," he is quoted as saying. Walter, "The Only Game in Town," p. 52.

29. Unsigned article in *New York Times*, January 8, 1970, p. 33.

30. Farley, quoted in Walter, "The Only Game in Town," p. 91.

31. Unsigned article in *New York Times*, November 3, 1971, p. 31.

32. See, for instance, New Jersey, *Public Hearings before Gambling Study Commission*, December 6, 1972. The arguments of Senator Musto, pp. 31-33, and of Gary Malamut of the Atlantic City Hotel-Motel Association, pp. 39A-45A, are of particular interest. Other hearings used in this chapter include New Jersey Senate, Judiciary Committee, *Gambling in Atlantic City, Public Hearing*, vols. 1-3, 1970; New Jersey Senate/Assembly, Judiciary Committees, *Gambling Games in Atlantic City, Public Hearings*, 1970; New Jersey Assembly, Judiciary, Law, Public Safety and Defense Committee, *Casino Gambling Public Hearing*, 1974; New Jersey Senate, Judiciary Committee, *Legalized Gambling Public Hearing*, 1973.

33. *New York Times*, February 11, 1972, p. 40.

34. Ibid., February 20, 1972, p. 29. Although the commission was bipartisan and contained citizen members, the most vocal members were proponents, including Musto, Dumont, and Pellecchia. They dominated the hearings and final report. See also ibid., July 27, 1972, p. 35.

35. Musto, though a Democrat from the northern part of the state, was a long-time ally of the Atlantic County machine.

36. New Jersey, *Public Hearings before Gambling Study Commission*, p. 22.

37. Ibid., p. 23. Musto's advocacy of gambling should also be seen within the context of other events in his life. In November 1977, he was charged for using his mayoral power in Union City to protect an illegal baccarat game. The

game was alleged to have been run at a bar owned by the wife of the former Union City police director. The case swiftly made its way through the courts before it was dismissed in March 1978 because the prosecution could not name a key informant. *New York Times*, November 18, 1977, II, p. 19; and March 31, 1978, p. 24. On May 10, 1981, Musto was sentenced to seven years in prison after having been found guilty of racketeering. The following day he was reelected mayor of Union City.

38. Ibid., pp. 35, 36.

39. Ibid., hearing held on December 6, 1972, pp. 2A.

40. Ibid., p. 3A.

41. New Jersey Gambling Study Commission, *Report to the Governor and Legislature* (Pursuant to SCR 58 [ORC] of 1972), February 5, 1973, pp. 15, 16.

42. Ibid., p. 35.

43. *New York Times*, March 13, 1973, p. 82; April 12, 1973, p. 94.

44. Ibid., December 7, 1973, p. 86.

45. Ibid., December 25, 1973, p. 44; January 9, 1974, p. 75.

46. Ibid., September 12, 1974, p. 81.

47. Ibid., September 19, 1974, p. 91.

48. New Jersey Election Board Enforcement Commission, Casino Gambling Referendum, Trenton, August 1977, p. 1.

49. *New York Times*, October 11, 1974, p. 84.

50. *The Press*, February 6, 1973; *New York Times*, October 14, 1974, p. 72.

51. *New York Times*, October 14, 1974, p. 72.

52. Ibid.

53. Ibid., October 26, 1974, p. 68; October 31, 1974, p. 87.

54. Ibid., November 6, 1974, p. 1.

55. James Cooper, quoted in *The Press*, October 12, 1974, p. 9.

56. Ibid., October 21, 1974, p. 1.

57. Robert Ford, quoted in *New York Times*, November 6, 1974, p. 31.

58. Wayne Dumont, quoted in *The Press*, November 7, 1974, p. 21.

59. Joseph Bradway, quoted in *New York Times*, November 7, 1974, p. 38.

60. Murray Raphel, quoted in ibid., November 10, 1974, p. 95.

61. Samuel Reider, quoted in ibid.

62. *New York Times*, September 10, 1975, p. 95.

63. Joseph McGahn, quoted in *The Press*, January 20, 1976, pp. 1, 8.

64. Howard Kupperman, quoted in ibid., February 26, 1976, p. 1.

65. Steven Perskie, quoted in ibid., p. 3.

66. Ibid., April 26, 1976, pp. 1, 11.

67. Frank Farley, quoted in ibid., April 18, 1976, p. 4.

68. Ibid., May 4, 1976, p. 1.

69. James Hurley, quoted in ibid., April 28, 1976, p. 14.

70. Angelo Errichetti, quoted in ibid., May 1, 1976, p. 10.

71. Article by Carlo Sardella in ibid., April 25, 1976, p. 1.

72. Joseph Job, quoted in ibid., p. 12.

73. Joseph Lazarow, quoted in ibid., May 21, 1976, p. 21.

74. Frank Farley, quoted in ibid.

75. Sanford Weiner, quoted in ibid., July 20, 1976, p. 1.

76. Geoffrey Douglas, "The Selling of Casino Gambling," *New Jersey Monthly*, January 1977, p. 23.

77. Sanford Weiner, quoted in ibid., p. 26.

78. Sanford Weiner, quoted in *The Press*, October 28, 1976, p. 30.

79. Ibid., November 2, 1976, p. 1.

80. *New York Times*, August 15, 1975, p. 45.

81. Ibid., September 14, 1976, p. 84; October 20, 1976, p. 95; October 21, 1975, p. 78.

82. CRNPTG, *Gambling in America*, appendix 1, pp. 74-75.

83. Michael Dorman, "Surrender in Atlantic City," *New Jersey Monthly*, May 1979, p. 46.

84. Sanford Weiner, quoted in *The Press*, November 7, 1976, p. 86.

85. Steven Perskie, quoted in Douglas, "The Selling of Casino Gambling," p. 25.

4. Rules and Reality

1. New Jersey Legislature, *Assembly State Government Committee Public Hearing on ACR-126*, April 14, 1976, p. 20.

2. *New York Times*, January 4, 1979, p. B2.

3. New Jersey Staff Policy Group on Casino Gambling, *Second Interim Report*, February 17, 1977, p. 5.

4. New Jersey State Government, Federal, and Interstate Relations Committee, *Public Hearing on Assembly Bill 2366* (Casino Control Act), December 15, 1976, Trenton (1977), p. 10.

5. Nevada Gaming Control Board, *Report on Gaming Control in New Jersey*, April 19, 1979, p. 2.

6. Staff Policy Group on Casino Gambling, *Second Interim Report*, p. 1.

7. *Staff Policy Group on Casino Gambling*, March 22, 1977, Legislative Draft, sections 80 and 84.

8. Ibid., p. 33.

9. Ibid., sections 80 and 84.

10. See comments of Jack Barense, in New Jersey, Legislature, *Public Hearing Before Assembly State Government Committee on Casino Control Act*, September 27, 1978.

11. New Jersey Legislature, *Public Hearing before the Senate Judiciary Committee on Senate Bill S1780*, March 2, 1977, pp. 15A-16A.

12. Confidential interview.

13. *Rouge et Noir, Resort Management Report*, December 24, 1979, p. 11.

14. *Gaming Business Magazine*, March 1980, p. 32.

15. Staff Policy Group on Casino Gambling, *Second Interim Report*, February 17, 1977.

16. Statement of Robert P. Martinez, special assistant to the attorney general. See New Jersey Legislature, *Assembly State Government Committee Public Hearing on Assembly Bill A1046*, March 13, 1978, p. 13.

17. Statement of John Degnan, attorney general, in ibid., p. 1.

18. Ibid.

19. Interview with Degnan in *New York Times*, February 13, 1980, as cited in *Rouge et Noir, Resort Management Report*, February 18, 1980, addendum, p. 14. On Resorts International see Gigi Mahon, *The Company That Bought the Boardwalk: A Reporter's Story of Resorts International* (New York: Random House, 1981).

20. *Rouge et Noir, Resort Management Report*, March 1979, addendum.

21. Ibid., November 1978.

22. "Atlantic City: The Wrong Ticket," *New York Times*, November 19, 1978.

23. New Jersey Legislature, *Assembly State Government Committee Public Hearing on Assembly Bill A 3318*, May 3, 1979.

24. Ibid.

25. See New Jersey Legislature, *Hearing on Assembly Bill A1081*, p. 17A.

26. Statement of Attorney General Degnan, ibid.

27. New Jersey Legislature, *Hearing on Assembly Bill A1201*, April 9, 1980.

28. Analysis prepared by Professor Richard Lehne, Rutgers University.

29. See New Jersey, *Legislative Index: 1980-81 Edition*, March 2, 1981, p. 7.

30. See New Jersey Legislature, *Hearing on Assembly Bill A1081*.

31. *Wall Street Journal*, July 21, 1981.

32. Ibid., July 13, 1981.

33. *Sunday Star Ledger*, July 19, 1981, sec. 1, pp. 8 and 26.

5. Employment

1. *The Press*, November 3, 1976, p. 1.

2. Statement by Robert List of Nevada in Laventhol and Horwath, *Second Annual Gaming Conference*, New York, October 1980, p. 21.

3. *The Press*, August 31, 1979, p. 1.

4. Ibid., March 30, 1980, p. 16.

5. Casino Control Commission, *Investigatory Hearings*, p. 288.

6. *Star Ledger*, May 19, 1981.

7. Department of Community Affairs (New Jersey), *Atlantic City Newsletter*, December 1, 1980.

8. *Star Ledger*, February 19, 1981.

9. *Wall Street Journal*, February 4, 1981, p. 1.

10. Ibid.

11. Casino Control Commission, *Investigatory Hearings*, p. 24.

12. Confidential interview.

13. *Star Ledger*, February 18, 1981.

14. Ibid., October 10, 1979, p. 6.

15. Confidential interview.

16. For welfare data, see New Jersey Department of Institutions and Agencies, Division of Public Welfare, *Annual Reports*, 1970-1981.

17. Interview with William Eames, Atlantic City Chamber of Commerce, January 29, 1981.

18. *Wall Street Journal*, June 26, 1981.

19. Casino Control Commission, *Investigatory Hearings*, p. 1.

20. Letter from Barbara Lampen, March 30, 1981.

21. *Rouge et Noir, Resort Management*, April 30, 1981.

6. Fiscal Realities

1. The following characteristics of the property tax system in New Jersey should be emphasized: *An ad valorem tax*. The local property tax is measured by property values and is apportioned among taxpayers according to the assessed value of taxable property owned by each taxpayer. The tax applies to real estate and tangible personal property of telephone and telegraph companies. *A local tax*. The property tax is a local tax assessed and collected by municipalities for the support of municipal and county governments and local school districts. No part of it is used for support of state government. *Amount of tax* (a residual tax). The amount of local property tax is determined each year, in each municipality, to supply whatever revenue is required to meet budgeted expenditures not covered by monies available from all other sources. School districts and counties notify municipalities of their property tax requirements. Municipalities add their own requirements and levy taxes to raise the entire amount. As a residual local tax, the total property tax is determined by local budgets and not by property valuations or tax rates. *Property assessment* (the tax base). All taxable property is assessed (valued for taxation) by local assessors in each municipality. Assessments are expressed in terms of "taxable value." See New Jersey, Local Property Tax, N.J.S.A. 54:4-1 et seq.

2. Alternatively, assessed valuation is termed taxable valuation or total assessments. The formal definitions are: *Taxable valuation*. The taxable valuation of a municipality is commonly referred to as the ratable base, and is comprised of real property and business personal property. These elements, in turn,

are defined as follows: *Real property*. The value of real property is the total taxable value of agricultural, residential, and industrial land (excluding railroad property which was removed from the local real-property tax base, effective in 1967), and the improvements thereon (e.g., buildings). *Business personal property*. This category refers to such property as machinery and production facilities. In New Jersey, only the business property of telephone, telegraph, and messenger system companies is assessed at the local level and taxed at the local rate, since the taxation of other business personal property was transferred to the state in 1968. After that date, "personal property used in business (other than the business of telephone, telegraph and messenger system companies) is subject to a uniform state tax instead of the local tax. Nonbusiness personal property is no longer subject to any property tax and inventories of all businesses were excluded from property taxation." See New Jersey, Department of the Treasury, Division of Taxation, *Annual Report* (Trenton, 1974), p. 57, for a review of definitions.

3. New Jersey, Department of the Treasury, Division of Taxation, *Annual Report* (Trenton, 1980), p. 32.

4. They are also used to allocate state school aid:

"Each year the Division of Taxation publishes a Table of Equalized Valuations showing the average ratio of assessed value to true value of real estate in each of the 567 local taxing districts. These tables are certified to the State Commissioner of Education pursuant to Chapter 86, Laws of 1954 (N.J.S.A. 54:1-35.1) for use in calculating and distributing State school aid. Equalized valuations are also the basis for apportioning county taxes among local taxing districts and for apportioning the tax cost of a large number of regional school districts among component taxing districts.

"Equalized valuations are also the basis for measuring debt limits for local governmental units.

"The ratio of assessed valuation to sales price is calculated for each usable sale and all are classified into four groups (vacant land, residential, farm, business). An overall district average weighted ratio is calculated for all classes as a weighted average of separate ratios calculated for each class. This district weighted ratio is applied against aggregate assessed value of the district to determine aggregate 'true value.' 'True value' is averaged with true value for the preceding year after adjustment for 'added and omitted assessments.' This averaging has the two-way advantage of avoiding abrupt changes in ratio from year to year and avoiding undue influence of inadequate samples of sales of a single year.

"The average ratio of assessed value to true value of all real estate in 1980 was 68.96 percent." Ibid., pp. 19 – 20.

5. This discussion and Table 17 relate only to real property as defined in note 2.

6. *Atlantic City Newsletter*, October 27, 1980, pp. 1-2.

7. Ibid., December 1, 1980, p. 6.

8. This is in part responsible for the increase in the municipal property-tax

levy for the past two years. See Table 16.

9. *Sunday Star Ledger*, May 24, 1981, p. 80.

10. It should be pointed out that this process is not unique to Atlantic City and the casino gaming industry. It appears to accompany many large-scale facility developments in New Jersey and elsewhere.

11. This levy, detailed in Chapter 4, involves 2 percent of gross win from casinos that have secured total gross profits in excess of their cumulative investment. The sole requirement of its expenditure is "investment in land development and housing in Atlantic or other counties to benefit the public good or to pay an equivalent tax to the state." At least as of this writing, the actual receipts of this tax are unclear, but certainly there is every indication that they are relatively small, with little direct support to Atlantic City to be anticipated from its expenditure.

12. Michael S. Serrill, "The Greening of Atlantic City," *Police Magazine*, November 1978.

13. Confidential interview.

14. Confidential interview.

15. *Atlantic City Newsletter*, December 1, 1980, p. 5.

16. Interview with Sonny Werblin, *Gaming Business Magazine*, September 1980, p. 5. Note also that the faltering of OTB in New York City has been attributed to the casinos competition.

17. Dean Witter Reynolds, *Gaming Abstract*, May 1979, p. 7.

18. Ibid., December 1980, p. 7.

7. Housing

1. While not totally prohibiting development, the constraints imposed are substantial. The draft management plan of the Pinelands commission, for example, defined the density zones up to 1 unit per 10 acres. Developers must meet other stringent requirements. See *A Review of the Impact on Residential Building in Atlantic County of Municipal Zoning and the Pinelands Management Plan* (Trenton: Department of Community Affairs, January 1981).

2. See George Sternlieb and James W. Hughes, *The Future of Rental Housing* (New Brunswick: Rutgers University Center for Urban Policy Research, 1981).

3. Atlantic City Housing Authority, *Survey*, 1979.

4. Casino Control Commission, *Investigatory Hearing Concerning the Development and Well-Being of Industries Within Atlantic City*, p. 233.

5. Bureau of the Census, 1980 Census of Population and Housing, *Advanced Report*, PHC80-V-32.

6. Casino Control Commission, *Investigatory Hearing*, p. 234.

7. Atlantic City Housing Authority, *Housing Inventory*, March 1980. For the earlier elements, see Atlantic City Planning and Development, *Atlantic City Housing Matrix*, n.d.

8. *The Press*, May 19, 1977, p. 25.

9. Ibid., October 8, 1977, p. 8.

10. Ibid., August 12, 1978, pp. 1, 8.

11. Ibid., March 2, 1978, pp. 1, 8.

12. Ibid., July 30, 1978, pp. 1, 6.

13. Ibid., December 8, 1978, p. 25.

14. Atlantic County Division of Economic Development, *Growth Trends Report: 1980 Annual Report*, pp. 7, 8.

15. Interview with Philip B. Caton, March 12, 1981.

16. Interview with Al Cade, March 2, 1981.

17. Interview with William G. Ferry, director, Board of Assessors, Atlantic City, February 23, 1981.

18. The pattern of land-value escalation is detailed in Chapter 6.

19. Francisco M. Troncaso, *Report of the Impact of Casino Gambling on the Welfare of the Poor, the Minorities and the Elderly in the Inlet Section of Atlantic City* (processed, Temple University), May 23, 1977, pp. 1-11.

20. *The Press*, September 15, 1978, pp. 1, 12.

21. Ibid., April 11, 1979, p. 1.

22. Ibid., January 15, 1981, pp. 1, 3.

23. Ibid., March 28, 1981, p. 14.

24. New Jersey Department of Community Affairs, *Atlantic City Newsletter*, October 27, 1980, p. 8.

25. Interview with Philip B. Caton, March 12, 1981.

26. Interview with Matthew McCool, February 19, 1981.

27. Interview with Pierre Hollingsworth, February 23, 1981.

28. Casino Control Commission, *Investigatory Hearing*, p. 1.

29. Ibid., p. 19.

30. Ibid., p. 27.

31. Ibid., p. 418.

32. Interview with Al Cade, March 2, 1981.

33. Interview with Barbara Lampen, March 12, 1981.

34. Interview with William Downey, March 29, 1981.

35. Interview with Al Cade, March 2, 1981.

36. See Sections 84E and 79 of the Casino Control Act.

37. Interview with Al Cade, March 2, 1981.

38. Confidential interview, March 26, 1981.

39. *Star Ledger*, February 19, 1981., p. 1.

40. *New York Times*, February 22, 1981, p. E6.

41. *Star Ledger*, February 19, 1981, p. 1.

42. Casino Control Commission, *Investigatory Hearing*, p. 176-177.

43. Ibid., p. 199.

44. Confidential interview, March 26, 1981.

45. Casino Control Commission, Investigatory Hearing, pp. 35-45.

46. Ibid., p. 7.

47. *Star Ledger*, May 22, 1981. p. 31.

48. Casino Control Commission, *Investigatory Hearing*, p. 275; *New York Times*, February 22, 1981.

49. Laventhol and Horwath, *First Annual Gaming Conference*, p. 37.

50. Casino Control Commission, *Investigatory Hearing*, p. 6.

51. Atlantic City Department of Planning, *Housing Matrix*, July 1982.

52. Confidential interview, March 20, 1981.

8. Crime

1. *Gambling Business*, August 1980, p. 19.

2. William Eadington, *The Economics of Gambling Behavior: A Qualitative Study of Nevada's Gambling Industry* (Reno: Bureau of Business and Economic Research, University of Nevada at Reno, 1973), p. 11.

3. Michael S. Serrill, "The Greening of Atlantic City," *Police Magazine*, November 1978, p. 24.

4. *Star Ledger*, March 18, 1981.

5. CRNPTG, *Gambling in America* (1976), p. 86.

6. We are greatful to Detective Beatrice K. Haynes of the Crime Analysis Unit of Atlantic City for making these facts available to us in advance of their formal publication.

7. *Philadelphia Inquirer*, January 25, 1981, p. A14.

8. Ibid., April 30, 1981, p. B3.

9. Ibid., January 25, 1981, p. A1.

10. Confidential interview.

11. Confidential interview.

12. State of New Jersey Commission of Investigation, *Report and Recommendations on the Incursion by Organized Crime in Certain Legitimate Businesses in Atlantic City* (Trenton, December 1977).

13. *Star Ledger*, April 16, 1981, p. 21.

14. Ibid.

15. Ibid., and *New York Times*, June 26, 1981, p. B4.

16. *Philadelphia Inquirer*, March 22, 1981, p. A1.

17. See special article by D. W. Nauss and Steve Twomey, *Philadelphia Inquirer*, December 21, 1980, p. A1.

18. *Philadelphia Inquirer*, April 27, 1981, p. A1.

19. *Star Ledger*, May 15, 1981, p. 1.

20. *Philadelphia Inquirer*, May 1, 1981, p. B1. The report itself is a font of information on organized crime and casinos. See Pennsylvania Crime Commission, *A Decade of Organized Crime, 1980 Report* (Philadelphia, 1980).

21 *Philadelphia Inquirer* December 21, 1980 p. A1. See also March 22, 1981, p. A1.

22. *New York Times*, February 24, 1981.

23. Ibid., June 26, 1981, p. B4.

24. For vivid background on Lansky and the origins of the financing of